Kirstie Allsopp
Craft

This book is dedicated to my mum, who has never once pulled a sickie and is slightly surprised that I can bake; and, as always, to Ben and the boys, my inspiration in everything and the light of my life.

Kirstie Allsopp
Craft

HODDER &
STOUGHTON

Contents

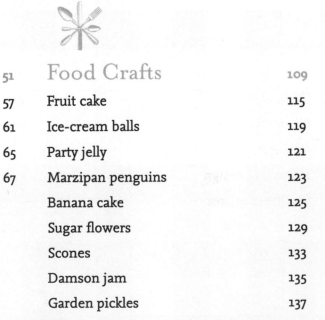

Garden Crafts

Gift Crafts

Flower Crafts

Contributors

Introduction

I began my love affair with British crafts a few years ago when I renovated my house in north Devon. I leapt at the chance to tempt everyone into the glorious world I discovered, where artisans and talented people make things by hand to love and last. You were inspired too – you joined craft groups, grabbed your granny's knitting needles, rummaged in your sewing basket and began making things for your home, your friends and family, and together we began a tidal wave of amazing crafting activity.

During the summer of 2011 I explored the wonderful world of crafts again and took to the road to visit some of the many county fairs and agricultural shows that take place up and down the country. I wanted to discover and celebrate the things that put our British crafting nation head and shoulders above the rest.

I love country shows. They're a celebration of our great British countryside and a brilliant day out to boot. They're perfect for packing a picnic and taking the kids to see the animals and play on the old-fashioned fairground rides. But some of my most memorable moments at shows have been on my own: at the Royal Cornwall Show I did ferret racing (my ferret lost); at the Devon County Show I was encouraged into a white boiler suit and rubber gloves to see inside a beehive; and at the Great Yorkshire Show I found myself sheep shearing in pink knee-high socks on a platform three metres above the ground. (Photos of the shows are dotted throughout this book.)

Ever since they began in the early nineteenth century, country shows have been the best place to find out about what's new – and old – in the countryside. If you want to keep chickens, learn how to make your own cider, or just find out more about country hobbies, they're the place to go. I also love the fact that all the local producers of foods, crafts and farming come together in one big field, so you can really find out what's

being made in your area. I'm not alone in my love for them as six million people visit these events every year.

Another great joy of country shows is that there are competitions for just about anything and everything. First there are the animals – thoroughbred horses, shampooed cattle, smoothly groomed sheep and incredibly dapper dogs – parading around show rings. Encircling these are show tents brimming with every craft competition you can imagine – from cushions to cakes, wine-making to embroidery, flower arranging to découpage and much, much more. They attract a talented army of home crafters, who take along their wares to be viewed and judged, each one of them hoping that theirs will be the winning entry. The diversity of ideas and crafts on show at these fairs is inspiring, and the skill that goes into them is self-evident. So, although pretty sure I couldn't beat them, I none-theless decided to join them and scare the living daylights out of myself in the process.

The aim was to use my existing skills and learn lots of new ones in an attempt to improve my crafting abilities and bring home the winner's rosette. Putting something you've made up for judging really pushes you to be the best you can, and if you're lucky enough to win, it's the best feeling in the world. I'm really pleased to say that I do now have some blue rosettes proudly displayed on my mantelpiece, and I even managed to get 'Best in Show' for one of my efforts. If, like me, you've got a passion for crafts, there's always a competition you can enter and I cannot recommend the experience highly enough.

To help me get up to scratch, I again enlisted the help of some of Britain's most talented and passionate crafts people. Sharing skills and encouraging others to learn and develop those skills is a proud part of the British crafting tradition: I really couldn't have achieved anything without their dedication, support and enthusiasm. They were truly inspiring and gave me the confidence to go for it.

In that tradition of sharing I hope this book opens your eyes to many new or different crafting skills and encourages you to learn and use them. Having been given the chance to turn my hand to a whole range of crafts, I can completely appreciate the skill, time and love that goes into every single one of them. Of course there are certain crafts that will always have a special place in my heart, but trying out different ones was absolutely fascinating and showed me that skills from one discipline can often be applied to others.

What I love most about crafts is that you don't have to be a great artist or skilled practitioner to make a success of them. If you can wield a pair of scissors, you can do paper crafts; if you can tell one colour from another, you can tackle flower arranging or machine embroidery. Disregard anything negative that people might have said in the past about your abilities; I guarantee there is a project here for you. All have been carefully chosen to present you with an enticing range of activities, and each takes you through the crafting process step by step. Whether you're a beginner or seasoned pro, I hope they prove that you can give everything a go and expect good results.

My love of all things British and the handmade has driven both the TV series and this book that accompanies it. Join me as I delve once again into the wonderful world of crafts, but be warned – it's addictive!

TOP TIPS FOR CRAFT FAIR COMPETITIONS

Read the rules. I know it sounds obvious, but however brilliant your entry, it will be marked down if it's not what they asked for.

Do something different. Judges often have to choose between twenty or thirty different entries, so try to give yours the wow factor. This doesn't necessarily mean extra work. For example, in an afternoon tea competition I used two chunky cake stands for my display, rather than traditional dainty ones, just to set my entry apart from the others.

Check out the opposition. Some competitions say no professionals, but in others you'll be up against the cream of the craft trade, so choose carefully and compete at a level that suits your skills.

Be crafty. Give your entry an unusual name to distinguish it from the others. In one baking competition, I added summery ingredients to my recipe and called the result a 'Caribbean fruit cake' to make sure the judges wouldn't compare it to all the Christmas cakes they'd eaten in the past.

Needlecrafts

When I was at school, I had to take home economics, which involved learning the basics of needlework – sewing, embroidery and crochet to name but a few. Over the years these skills made their way to the back of my mind. Yes, I could sew on a button or mend a hole in a pair of school trousers, but I wanted to be able to do more than that. Now, years later, thanks to many of my inspirational crafting friends, I have rediscovered all these skills and more, and I haven't looked back. It turns out they were simply tucked away in the far recesses of my brain.

If you too have forgotten the arts of needlecraft, delve deep in your own recesses and I'm sure you will rediscover them too. Like riding a bike, the techniques come back to you, and although you may be rusty to start with, a bit of practice will soon have you in full swing. To those of you for whom the passion has never gone away, I commend you for your commitment to the cause. In this chapter, I hope that no matter what level you are at, whether a complete beginner, a re-starter or an expert looking for new projects, you will find something to suit.

Needlework of all kinds has made its way back into our consciousness and shaken off its old-fashioned image. Maybe it's because in these cash-strapped times we've all taken up make do and mend, or maybe it's because modern design and thinking have embraced needlecraft, allowing us to take a fresh look at things. Possibly it's a combination of the two, but, whatever the reason, I am delighted to say that needlework is back with a vengeance and bigger and better than ever.

SEWING   When I was growing up, loads of mums had sewing machines at home but in my generation it was out of vogue to own one. Luckily, that has all changed in the last few years. I went out and bought my sewing machine after a refresher session with a family friend rekindled my passion, and it turns out I wasn't the only one. Sewing machines have been flying off the shelves. It just shows that more than ever we are rejecting our throw-away society in favour of making and recycling, and to my mind, sewing is one of the best ways you can do this.

The sewing machine, first patented in 1790 by Thomas Saint, has come a long way over the years. Its invention for home use meant that women who considered sewing part of the drudgery of domestic life were liberated. Today the home sewing machine is all singing, all dancing, and can do just about anything you would ever want or need it to (sewing wise, that is), and sewing as a hobby has become hugely popular again. If you are thinking about buying a machine, do as I advise my house buyers: look around, do your research, ask the experts loads of questions, and buy the best you can afford. If you are planning to sew just a few simple home projects or take in a skirt, a basic machine will fit the bill; but if you feel that in future you might want to progress to something more demanding, such as quilting, it might be worth investing in a more sophisticated model now rather than having to buy a whole new machine a few years down the line. Remember, though, that even basic machines can usually be added to later (you can buy extra feet for different jobs). Once you get your foot on the pedal, you might never want to stop. I know I didn't.

But for me, sewing isn't just about the practicalities of saving money on a pair of curtains for your home or mending a ripped pair of trousers; it's about creating something with love. From soft furnishings to clothing and beyond, there is so much you can do with a sewing machine. When I sit at mine I really do feel that the world is my oyster. The possibilities are endless.

For a good starter project, try out the vintage bunting on page 17, which combines my love of sewing and vintage fabrics. It will brighten up the house during the winter and look amazing in the garden throughout the summer.

EMBROIDERY I'm passionate about embroidery, both the hand and machine varieties. (I think I once even described machine embroidery as the crack cocaine of the crafting world. Yes, it's that addictive!) Added to that, it's also one of the most social crafts I've come across. There are groups meeting up and down the country every week, and these are a great place to get started if you've never done embroidery before. As with crafting groups in all disciplines, there is always a more experienced crafter ready and willing to share their knowledge.

Hand embroidery is a centuries-old skill steeped in tradition. It was sometimes used to tell wonderful stories (think of the Bayeux Tapestry), but, more often than not, its purpose was simply to make fabrics look pretty. In the eighteenth century embroidery was considered an essential skill for any society lady worth her salt, and the advent of luxurious materials and threads meant the craft thrived in these circles. Gradually, it became more widespread, and in 1904 the Embroiderers Guild was founded. Today it has more than 25,000 members, so embroidery is certainly alive and kicking.

Machine embroidery is a relatively new skill, but growing fast. It can be done on any sewing machine – all you have to do is buy an embroidery foot – but most modern home machines now offer various embroidery stitches as standard.

I have included two embroidery projects in this chapter – a beautiful handkerchief design for the hand embroiderers amongst you (page 29) and a table runner for the machine enthusiasts (page 33).

If straightforward embroidery doesn't float your boat, turn to page 45 for another form of embroidery – cross-stitch, which is done on an even-weave fabric or canvas. This craft really took off in 1804, when a print seller in Germany began to develop blocked and coloured patterns for mass production. By 1840, over 14,000 designs were available in the UK, but the craft gradually went into decline, until war work knocked it on the head in the twentieth century. It was in the 1960s that cross-stitching began to perk up again. Since then, the craft has gone from strength to strength and today it's hugely popular.

QUILTING I shout about the glory of quilts from the rooftops whenever I can. I absolutely adore them. They combine history, artistic talent and skill, and every single one has a story to tell both in the fabric and the making. Each one takes time, love and effort to complete, so each is a unique work of art and that's what makes them so special.

Ever since I received my first pay packet I have been buying and collecting quilts, particularly vintage ones, and I'm always on the lookout for them. One of my purchases, a vintage American quilt I found in an antique shop, provided the starting point for one of the bedrooms at Meadowgate, my cottage in Devon, and the kids' room is completed by a quilt that was especially made for me. The latter is now a family heirloom, and that's another reason to love quilts – they are made to last. Use them, love them and treat them well and they will last a lifetime and beyond.

There are two types of quilt: decorative and utilitarian. Historically, upper-class women had lots of leisure time and access to fine fabric, so they tended to own and produce beautiful decorative quilts. It's said that Henry VIII (who had a huge collection of gold and silver quilts) gave his fifth wife, Katherine Howard, twenty-three embroidered quilts as a sign of his favour – lucky lady! Working-class women, on the other hand, produced coarser and more utilitarian quilts because they needed warm, inexpensive bed covers.

Making a quilt can be one of the most rewarding crafts there is, but it does take time and commitment. As many quilters will tell you, the basics are simple, but you never stop learning as there are endless techniques. The quilt on page 41 uses the stack and whack technique, which is great for beginners as it produces fast results. If you want more of a challenge, try the lovely appliqué cushion on page 21, which combines quilting with machine embroidery – a winning combination in my view.

KNITTING I never really got the hang of knitting when I was young. My left-handedness always got in the way, but I was lucky enough to learn again a couple of years ago and I now have a huge appreciation of the talent and skill involved in this versatile craft.

Over the last few decades, knitting has had a rocky ride. It fell out of vogue in the 1980s, when sales of yarn and patterns slumped, but I'm pleased to say that it has made a major comeback. There are now hundreds of knitting groups up and down the country, and it's estimated by the UK Hand Knitting Association that there are between four and seven million knitters in the UK, with new converts being made all the time. Given the beautiful yarns and gorgeous books now available, that statistic comes as no surprise to me.

If you want to take up knitting but don't know where to start, my best advice is to join a group. Ask in your local knitting shop or search online, and soon you'll be making fantastic modern patterns, such as the coasters on page 39.

Vintage Bunting

I love vintage fabrics of any kind. It's an addiction I just can't control. I've got bags full of vintage scraps in my cupboard and I'm always on the lookout for projects to reinvent these beautiful pieces. Now, thanks to crafter Mandy Shaw, I've found the solution with this fabulous vintage bunting. It can be adapted for any occasion, made to any length you like, and will add a bit of colour all year round both inside and out.

YOU WILL NEED

- Pencil and ruler
- Cardboard
- Scissors
- Vintage fabrics (old clothes, curtains, tablecloths, etc.)

- Spray starch
- Plain fabric, for the backing
- Pins
- Sewing needle and thread
- Sewing machine

- Pinking shears (optional)
- Size oo piping cord, for threading flags
- Sellotape

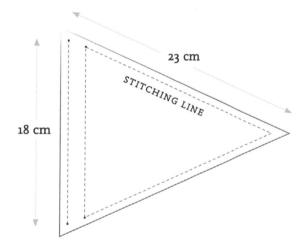

1. Draw a triangle on your cardboard with the dimensions shown above. Cut around the shape.
2. Spread out your vintage fabric, spray starch all over it and press with an iron.
3. Place the triangle template on your vintage fabric and trace around it in pencil to make as many triangles as you need. (Eight will make 2 metres of bunting.) These pieces will be the front of your bunting, so make sure you place the template on the best parts of your fabric. This will mean that some of your flags will not be cut on the straight grain, but don't worry – we'll deal with that later. Cut out each triangle.
4. Now cut out a second cardboard triangle 2.5 cm bigger all round than the first one. Place this on the plain fabric and cut out the same number of triangles as you have made with your vintage fabric. (Your vintage triangles will be very stretchy if they haven't been cut on the straight grain, so the plain fabric triangles are cut a bit bigger to cope with that stretchiness in the next step.)

5. Pin a plain triangle to a vintage triangle, wrong sides together, leaving an open channel about 2.5 cm wide below the short edge. Stitch around the long sides up to the channel and then straight across below the channel, keeping the needle about 1.5 cm from the outside edge. Now stitch the short side above the channel.

6. Trim the flag with pinking shears or fray the edges with your fingers. Make all the other flags in the same way.

7. Cover the ends of the piping cord with Sellotape and thread it through the open channel in the flags. Tie a knot in each end to prevent the cord slipping out.

8. Arrange the flags along the cord about 7.5–10 cm apart, leaving 50 cm of cord at each end. When you are happy with the arrangement, stitch both sides of each flag to the cord.

9. Spray starch on the flags again, then hang up your bunting and admire your handiwork.

TOP TIPS

• If your vintage fabric is embroidered, take care to centralise the embroidery within the template for the best effect on each flag.

• As cutting paper tends to blunt scissors, it's a good idea to keep one pair for using exclusively with fabric.

• Place pins horizontally on the stitching line and the machine foot can go straight over them. Remove when the stitching is complete.

5

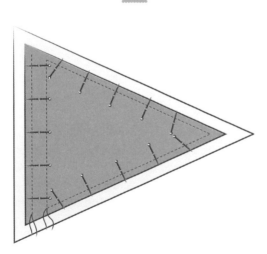

6

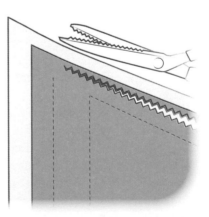

Appliqué Cushion

There's definitely a touch of magic about this lovely cushion, which ace crafters Jo Colwill and Linda Miller taught me how to make. In fact, for me it feels like winning the lottery because it incorporates several crafts that I really love – patchwork, quilting, embroidery and appliqué.

Linda began by showing me how to make a machine-embroidered Yorkshire rose on special fabric that simply disappears to leave just your stitching. That's enough in itself to give me a warm glow of achievement, but it just gets better. Jo then showed me how to make a block of patchwork, which I hand-embroidered, appliquéd and quilted, before turning it into a cushion scented with lavender.

I entered my cushion into the needlecraft competition at the Great Yorkshire Show and was astonished and humbled at how well I did in the face of fierce competition. I have to say, I'm very proud of my creation. The finished cushion is 28 cm square.

FOR THE APPLIQUÉ ROSE YOU WILL NEED

- Scissors
- Soluble base fabric (resembles waxy paper and dissolves in water)
- Embroidery hoop, preferably wooden
- Tracing paper and pencil
- Air-soluble pen (optional)
- Sewing machine with size 80 needle and embroidery foot
- Machine embroidery thread, in appropriate colours
- Hairdryer

1. Cut a 15–20 cm square of soluble base fabric and place it in your embroidery hoop.
2. Trace the rose below, then use pencil or an air-soluble pen to transfer the design to the fabric in the hoop.

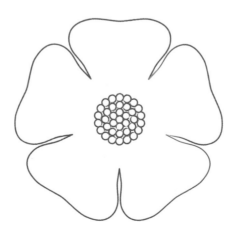

3. Put the sewing machine into 'ordinary sewing tension', then thread it up with embroidery thread.
4. Place the hoop under the needle, then put your foot on the pedal and move the hoop to create your stitches, following the lines of your design and filling the petals with stitching. Change your thread colour as appropriate. Once all the stitching is completed, take the fabric out of the hoop.
5. Place the work in a bowl of warm water and all the fabric will disappear, leaving only the machine embroidery. Dry with a hairdryer and set aside while you make the cushion.

FOR THE CUSHION
YOU WILL NEED

· ·

- 4 scraps of vintage fabric, one for each season
- Tape measure
- Paper and pencil
- Scissors or a rotary cutter, with cutting mat and ruler
- Pins
- Sewing machine
- Thread to match your fabric
- 60 x 50 cm piece of linen, for inner border and back of cushion
- Fabric for outer border (a small floral design is good)
- Tracing paper
- Freezer paper, waxed on one side (or use the wrapping around photocopy paper, which is waxed on the inside)
- Fabric for the hare design, plus matching thread
- Small fabric scissors (optional)
- Small appliqué needle
- Bondaweb (optional)
- Embroidery thread in green, red, yellow and white
- Embroidery needle (any large-eye sewing needle will do)
- Very small mother-of-pearl buttons and/or tiny beads
- 30 cm square of plain calico
- 30 cm square of cotton wadding
- 505 Temporary Adhesive spray (optional)
- Waxed thread for hand quilting, or 50/2 thread for machine quilting
- Sewing machine with open-toe darning foot
- 30 cm strip of lace, broderie anglaise or frill
- 30 cm cushion pad
- Dried lavender, sewn into a little muslin sachet

Note: A seam allowance needs to be added all round when cutting squares and strips. The usual allowance is 6 mm, but do check that your machine foot matches this. Align the foot with the edge of your fabric, then measure from the needle to the fabric edge. Whatever the distance is should be the width of the seam allowance you add.

PATCHWORK AND BORDERS

1. Spread out your vintage fabrics and draw a 5 x 5 cm square on each one. Add a 6 mm seam allowance all round, then cut out. Pin two squares right sides together, machine along one side, then press the seam flat in one direction. Repeat with the other two squares. Sew the pairs together, making sure their seams point in opposite directions. Press the long seam open.

2. Now take your linen and mark out four strips for borders:

       1) 10 x 5 cm
       2) 15 x 5 cm
       3) 15 x 10 cm
       4) 25 x 10 cm

   Add a 6 mm seam allowance all round each strip, then cut out.

3. With right sides together, pin and stitch border 1 along one side of your patchwork. Press the seam inwards.

4. Continuing in a clockwise direction, stitch borders 2, 3 and 4 to the patchwork in the same way. The patchwork will be slightly off-centre, but this is deliberate to leave space for the hare and rose appliqués.

5. Using your floral fabric, mark out two strips 2 x 25 cm. Add 6 mm seam allowance all round, then cut out and sew to the top and bottom of your patchwork. Now mark out two strips 2 x 28 cm. Add a 6 mm seam allowance all round, then cut out. Sew these pieces to the sides of your patchwork. Press the seams towards the outside to make a raised border.

1

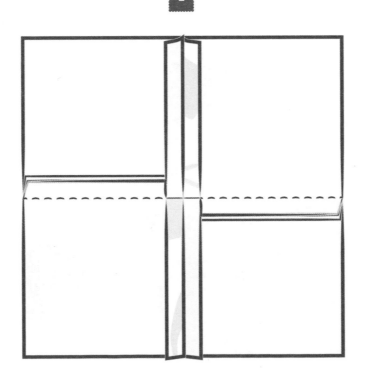

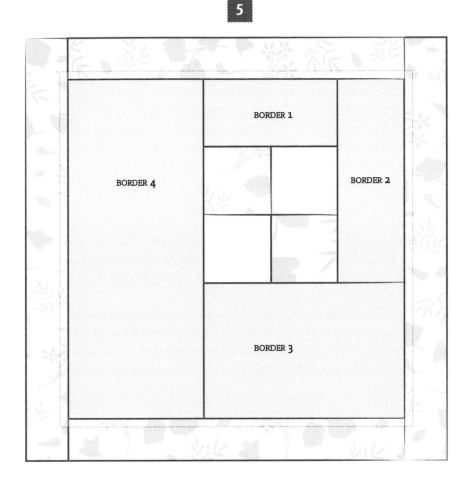

HARE APPLIQUE

6. Now trace around the hare design below. Place the freezer paper shiny side down, transfer the tracing to it and cut out the shape.

7. Place the wax paper hare, shiny side down, on the right side of your chosen fabric and press with an iron. Lightly pencil an extra 4 mm seam allowance all round, then cut out the hare shape, using small, sharp fabric scissors for greatest accuracy.

8. Place the hare on your cushion, paper side up. Fold the seam allowance under the template and pin in place. Now use matching thread and a small appliqué needle to sew around the hare with small hand stitches close to the edge. Jo recommends sewing from right to left, starting at the top of an ear and working along the back of the hare. For a quicker result, it's possible to Bondaweb appliqué (see page 33), but sewing around it gives the motif a lovely finish and your stitches get better and better with practice.

9. Put the appliquéd work face down on a towel and iron the back (if you iron it on the front, it will create marks). Turn over, peel off the paper template and voilà – an appliqué hare!

EMBROIDERY

10. Now it's time to create your border of embroidered flowers. My cushion has them scattered down the left-hand side and along the bottom. Using stem stitch and a variety of green threads, sew lots of flower stems in different heights (don't pull too tight or the fabric will pucker). Add the leaves in chain stitch.

11. The flower heads can be made in various ways. For small ones, make French knots. For bigger ones make petals in chain stitch with a French knot in the middle, or sew on small buttons with a yellow cross-stitch. Or even make some small water-soluble daisies (see technique, page 21) and catch these down in the centre with a bead or a French knot.

STEM STITCH   CHAIN STITCH   FRENCH KNOT

12. Once you have embroidered as many flowers as you want, decide where to put the appliqué rose and attach it in the centre with French knots or tiny beads. This leaves the petals loose, which creates lovely texture and shadow.

QUILTING

13. Lay the calico square on your work surface, place the cotton wadding over it, and sit the cushion front on top, right side up. Pin, tack or spray with 505 Temporary Adhesive to sandwich all three layers together.

CUSHION BACK

14. Now you are ready to quilt these layers by sewing around the outline of the rose and the shapes on the patchwork. If hand quilting, use waxed thread, which is stronger than

ordinary thread, and make little running stitches. If machine quilting, use an open-toe darning foot and 50/2 thread so that the stitches sink into the fabric rather than standing proud. The idea is to use the machine needle like a pencil to 'draw' your design.

15. When you are satisfied with your quilting, make the envelope opening on the back of the cushion. Spread out the remaining linen and mark out two pieces – one 16.5 x 29 cm, and another piece 11.5 x 29 cm. Add a 6 mm seam allowance all round, then cut out.

16. Sew a double hem along one long edge of the smaller piece. On the other piece, place a strip of lace along one long edge, right sides together, and sew a 6 mm seam. Press the seam flat to the wrong side so the lace projects about 1 cm beyond the folded edge.

17. Pin the lace-edged piece to the quilted front of the cushion, right sides together. Pin the other piece on top with the hemmed edge overlapping the lace. Machine around the raw edges, reinforcing at the corners and where the back pieces overlap by reversing over two stitches before stitching onwards. Clip the corners and turn right side out. Finally, you have to 'stitch in the ditch', about 6 mm from the seam between the linen border and the outer floral border, to clarify the edge detail.

18. Insert the cushion pad and the lavender sachet, if using, and your cushion is finished.

TOP TIPS

• Air soluble pens are a great option if you want to make a quick-fading mark on your fabric. The mark will last 1–24 hours.

• A size 80 needle is a good general-purpose size for machine embroidery, but remember, the thicker the fabric, the thicker the needle required.

• A rotary cutter offers quick and very accurate cutting, which is essential in quilting, so it's worth investing in one if you plan to make several quilts. Always use with a self-healing rotary cutting mat to protect the work surface and prolong the life of the rotary cutting blade. And always cut against a patchwork ruler with a lip, not an ordinary metal or plastic ruler.

Embroidered Handkerchief

Hand embroidery is one of Britain's most popular crafts, and I can see why. It's intricate, detailed and a really fulfilling way to spend a few hours. In a world full of multi-tasking, interruptions and information overload, it can be a great way to take time out, focus on one thing and unwind.

If you're new to embroidery, this delightful project, designed by Amanda Walker, is a great place to start. It uses just a few simple stitches, yet produces the most beautiful results. Once you've mastered the basics, you can apply embroidery to all sorts of things – pillowslips, baby clothes, even greeting cards – and discover that embroidery today is fresh and fabulous.

YOU WILL NEED

- White handkerchief
- Pencil
- 10 cm embroidery hoop
- Scissors
- 6-stranded cotton embroidery thread,
- in Pink 203, Dark pink 867, Lime green 6115, Green 207
- Embroidery needle

1. Photocopy the template below to the size you want, then lay it underneath a corner of the handkerchief and trace the design onto the fabric using a hard sharp pencil. The pencil line will later be covered by the embroidery.
2. Lay the corner over the inner ring of the embroidery hoop, then press the outer ring over it. Adjust the tension screw so that the fabric is smooth and taut (see Top Tips).
3. Cut a length of pink thread, remove two strands from the six, and thread your needle with them. You will start by embroidering a petal in fishbone stitch, so make a small stitch at the centre top of the petal, then make overlapping filling stitches, angling your needle up to one side from the centre and then to the other side until all the petal shape has been filled. Fill the four remaining petals in the same way.

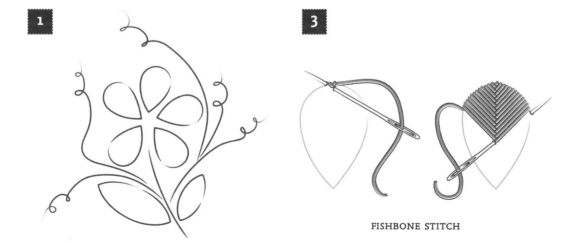

FISHBONE STITCH

4. Now you are going to make 5–10 French knots in the centre of the flower. These can be made alternately in dark pink and lime green. Thread your needle with one strand of your chosen colour and bring the needle to the right side. Wind the thread around the needle twice, twist the needle back on itself and insert it close to the starting point before repositioning for the next knot (see illustration, page 26).

5. Using one strand of the dark pink thread, complete the centre of the flower by making three vertical stitches at the base of each petal: this will define the outer two edges and the centre of each petal.

6. Next fill the leaf shapes with open fishbone stitch. Using two strands of the green thread, bring the needle out just below the top point of the leaf, insert it to the right at a slight upward angle, carry the thread across the back, and bring it out at the left side of the leaf. Make a downward-sloping small stitch in the centre of the leaf, then repeat the process from 'insert it to the right' until the whole leaf shape has been filled.

7. Work the stem of the flower in two strands of green thread in stem stitch (see page 26). Working from left to right along the pencil line, keep the thread to the left of the needle and make small even stitches.

8. Using one strand of the lime green thread, work a backstitch along the twirled lines. At the tips of these lines make one French knot (see page 26) in dark pink, then surround this knot with pink French knots.

9. Remove the hoop and press the handkerchief on a padded surface with a damp cloth.

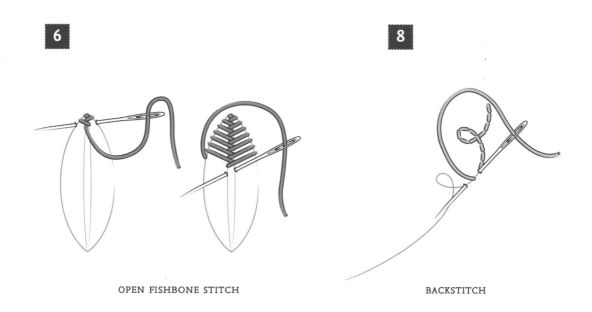

OPEN FISHBONE STITCH   BACKSTITCH

TOP TIPS

• To avoid using knots in your thread, lay the starting thread under the working area and it will be secured while stitching. To finish, weave the finishing thread through the reverse stitches on the back of your work.

• If working on fine fabrics, it is a good idea to bind the inner ring of your embroidery hoop with cotton tape. This helps to grip the fabric and prevent it being damaged.

• A magnifying glass is always a help when hand embroidering. Craft shops stock many different types, including ones that hang from your neck or clamp to the table.

Table Runner

I'm often asked what my favourite craft is, but I've never been willing to put my neck on the line and choose. That was before Amanda Walker introduced me to machine embroidery, which I can boldly state is one of the best crafts ever. I love it. It's totally addictive, and once you get going, believe me, you won't be able to stop.

One of the best things about machine embroidery is that you can do it with any kind of sewing machine. Just attach a quilting or embroidery foot, drop the feed dogs (the teeth below the needle, which help to move the fabric through) and you're away. You can machine-embroider almost any type of fabric, from scraps of ribbon, net and lace to much heavier wool and canvas. However, if you are a novice to embroidery, it's a good idea to start with more stable fabrics, such as cotton poplins and silk dupion. Whatever you choose, you can embroider it with any design you like, and the results are astonishing.

I love this project for a table runner. It's fun, practical and most of all it's a manageable and creative introduction to machine embroidery. Note that it uses Bondaweb to appliqué or attach one piece of fabric to the other. If you haven't used Bondaweb before, just follow the guide below. It really is as easy as pie.

YOU WILL NEED

- Scraps of green and pink silk fabric
- Ruler
- Pencil
- Scissors

- Bondaweb
- 1 plain ready-made runner in whatever fabric and size you like (available from stores such as John Lewis)

- Pink and green machine embroidery thread
- Sewing machine with a quilting foot

HOW TO USE BONDAWEB

Bondaweb is a very fine, web-like material with a paper backing. It is often used for appliqué, a technique that involves applying fabric shapes to another piece of fabric.

1. Take a piece of fabric from which you intend to cut your shapes.
2. Cut out enough Bondaweb to fit that piece of fabric.
3. Place the Bondaweb, with the paper backing uppermost, on the wrong side of the fabric and press with an iron. This sticks it to the fabric.
4. Draw the shapes you want on the paper backing, then cut them out.
5. Peel off the backing, then turn the shape over and position it on the base fabric to which you want to attach it. Press with an iron to stick it in place.

1. Spread out your scraps of fabric. Measure out five 12 cm squares on the green fabric, and five 6 cm squares on the pink fabric. Cut them out and fray the edges of all these squares.

2. Cut a 5 cm square of Bondaweb. Place it on the wrong side of a pink square with the paper backing uppermost and press with an iron. Peel off the backing, turn the square over and position it in the centre of a green square. Use the iron to stick the pink square to the green.

3. Now cut an 11 cm square of Bondaweb and iron this to the back of the green square. Peel off the backing paper, position the square in the centre of the runner and iron it in place.

4. Repeat steps 2 and 3 to attach the remaining squares equally along the runner.

5. Thread the machine with green embroidery thread, attach the quilting foot and drop the feed dogs. Start stitching in the centre of one of the pink squares. Allow the needle to remain static for a few stitches; this will prevent the stitching from unravelling. Next use your hands to manipulate the direction of the stitching; make a line of stitching out towards the edge of the pink square; at the end of this line remain static for a few stitches. Cut the thread and return to the beginning of the line and make another line of stitching close to the first. This stitching doesn't need to be perfect. Continue making double lines of stitching from the centre of the square to create a star effect. Do not cut the threads at the beginning of each stitching line: these are left to create a soft, feathery effect.

6. Change the thread to pink. Using the pink thread, extend each of the green stitching lines out into the green square. At the end of the double pink line make a dot by circling around and around. Cut the threads at both ends of these lines. Continue extending the green lines in pink and making dots at the end of then until a dandelion head has been formed. Repeat on the four remaining pink and green squares.

TOP TIPS

• The best thing to remember when machine-embroidering is to relax. There is no right or wrong; all your stitches are part of the design, and mistakes can lead to something that you would never have thought of, so free your mind.

• If you're feeling adventurous, or can't find a ready-made runner to your liking, simply make your own in the fabric of your choice. Hem it neatly before you start embroidering, and mitre the corners if you want it to look professional.

2

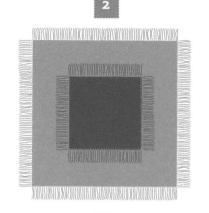

4

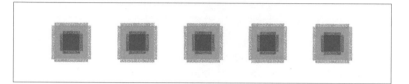

5

6

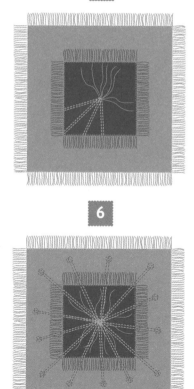

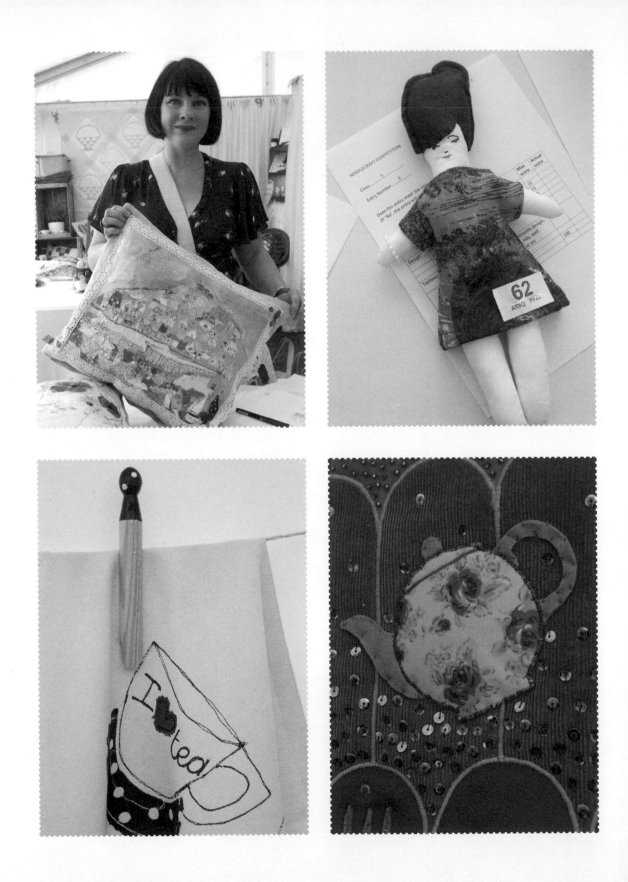

Bubble Coasters

These pretty coasters, designed by knitting expert Suzie Johnson, are simple to make. They are worked in stocking stitch (knit a row, purl a row) and the finished size is 13.5 x 13.5 cm.

YOU WILL NEED

- 2 pairs knitting needles, 3.75 mm and 3.25 mm
- 1 x 50 g ball yellow DK (for background – Yarn A)
- 1 x 50 g ball green DK (for 'bubbles' – Yarn B)
- 1 x 50 g ball raspberry DK (for edging – Yarn C)
- 1 x 50 g ball pink DK (for edging – Yarn D)
- Sewing needle and thread

KEY: DK = DOUBLE KNIT   STS = STITCHES   INC = INCREASE

1. Using the 3.75 mm needles and Yarn A, cast on 27sts.
2. Starting with a knit row, work 4 rows in stocking stitch in Yarn A.
3. Follow the chart below, introducing Yarn B as indicated, until all 33 rows have been worked.
4. Cast off in Yarn A purlwise.
5. Sew in all the ends. Cover the coaster with a damp cloth and press with a cool iron.
6. Now you need to knit the edging. Using the 3.25 mm needles and Yarn C, *pick up and knit 27sts along the top edge of the coaster with the right side facing. Continue as follows: Row 1: Knit. Row 2: Inc 1, knit to last st, inc 1 (29). Row 3: Knit. Row 4: Inc 1, knit to last st, inc 1 (31). Row 5: Knit. Row 6: Inc 1, knit to last st, inc 1 (33). Row 1: Knit. Cast off.*
7. Repeat from * to * down the left edge of the coaster in Yarn C.
8. Repeat from * to * on the bottom edging and up the right side edging using Yarn D.
9. Sew in all ends, then join corners together. With the wrong side up, cover the knitting with a damp cloth and press again with the iron.

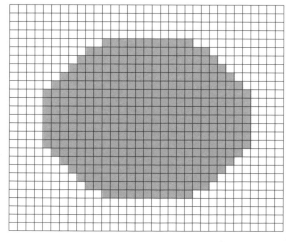

Coaster chart (each square represents 1 stitch)

❧ Stack and Whack Quilt ❧

My love of quilts has no bounds. To me, they are the most amazing pieces that combine the skill of sewing with love, care and attention. Of course, they take time and effort, but what could be more fulfilling than seeing the end result?

This quirky quilt, designed by Mandy Shaw, uses the stack and whack technique, which was originally developed as an easy way to create quilt blocks with a unique kaleidoscope design. Rather than cutting each piece of your quilt individually, you layer and cut a 'stack' of fabric and then 'whack' it together by hand or machine. The finished size is roughly 121 x 121 cm.

YOU WILL NEED

- A3 paper (newspaper is fine)
- Ruler and felt tip pen
- Scissors
- 10 'fat quarters' – a patch working term for pieces of fabric 56 x 46 cm – with large prints or unusual textures (brocade, corduroy, velvet, etc.)
- Pins
- Rotary cutter (with a cutting mat and ruler), or scissors
- Sewing machine, ideally with a walking foot attachment (the foot is optional, but produces a better result)
- Sewing thread
- Contrasting fabric,
- 110 x 30 cm, for sashing (the border around the blocks)
- Masking tape (optional)
- Fleece fabric, 150 x 150 cm, for backing
- 100 safety pins
- Contrasting fabric, 110 x 50 cm, for binding
- Sewing needle

All seam allowances have been added.

1. To make your paper pattern, draw a 40.5 cm square on newspaper with a felt tip pen and cut out. Copy the block pattern below onto the square, numbering each shape as indicated. Make two more patterns in the same way.
2. Iron all your fabric, then make two stacks of five pieces, right sides up (this is very important). Pin a paper pattern on the top layer of each stack, placing it in one of the corners to maximise the use of fabric.

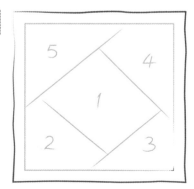
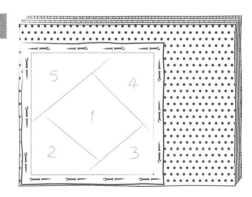

3. Using a rotary cutter or large scissors, cut around the pattern square, then cut into the individual shapes. This can be tricky because of the thickness, but it doesn't need to be completely accurate at this stage. Make sure you keep the shapes in their correct places.

4. Remove the pattern pieces, but keep them nearby in their original arrangement to refer to as a guide. Set aside all the leftover fabric for the final border.

5. The next task is to prepare your stacks of shapes and is most important, so take your time. When you take the fabrics off the stack, they must stay in the order that you took them off and all fabrics must have right side facing up. Here goes:

   Stack 1 – ignore
   Stack 2 – take one fabric off the top and put it underneath the stack.
   Stack 3 – take two fabrics off the stack and put them underneath.
   Stack 4 – take three fabrics off the top and put them underneath.
   Stack 5 – take four fabrics from the top and put them underneath.

6. Now label each stack 1, 2, 3, 4, 5 in sequence with a scrap of paper and a pin.

7. Repeat steps 5 and 6 with the other set of squares.

8. Put the two sets of cut-up squares still in their stacks on a tray, keeping them in their original arrangement, and head for the sewing machine.

9. Take a piece of fabric from the top of stacks 1 and 2 and sew right sides together with a 6 mm seam. You are aiming to replicate the 1–5 arrangement you have drawn up, so refer to the paper pattern to see which edges you should sew. Stitch to this a piece from stack 3, then a piece from stack 4, and finally a piece from stack 5. This will form one block. At this stage, the pieces may look uneven and not square, but don't worry as they will be cut to size later.

10. Repeat step 9 for all the pieces, remembering to follow the numbers at all times, until all the blocks are sewn together.

11. When you have sewn the two sets of five stacks you should end up with ten different. blocks. Press each individual block and cut to exactly 32 x 32 cm.

12. Join nine blocks together in three rows of three, making sure that different fabrics are next to each other (see illustration 14). You might have to twist and turn them to get this right. Sew together with a consistent seam of 6 mm. Remember, one block will be left over.

13. Take your sashing material and cut into four strips each 5 cm wide across the width of the fabric. With right sides together, pin and stitch a strip to the top and bottom of your patchwork blocks, then press the seam open with an iron. Pin, stitch and press the other two strips to the sides of the patchwork in the same way.

14. To create the border around the sashing, cut the leftover scraps of material into strips 10 cm wide and join them together in a random manner to make a long strip. Press the seams open. With right sides together, pin and stitch these patchwork strips to the outer edge of the sashing. Press the seams open.

15. Pin or tape your fleece to the carpet or floor, wrong side up. Put your patchwork piece on top, right side up. Pin both layers together with safety pins, especially around the edges, placing a pin every 7.5 cm.

16. Using a walking foot attachment if you have one, machine the two layers together, first around the patchwork area, then around the outer edge of the sashing. Also stitch around the central piece of each block.

17. Now cut your binding fabric into five strips 6 cm wide. Join them together in one continuous length and press the seams open. Fold the whole strip in half lengthways and press.

18. Pin the binding along one side of your quilt, right sides together and raw edges matching. Starting 7.5 cm from the beginning of your binding, and sewing 6 mm from the raw edge, stitch until you reach one corner, stopping 6 mm from the end – this is very important. Lift the needle and pull the work away from the machine, leaving the thread still attached. Fold the binding up and away from you towards the north, so that it is aligned with the edge of the quilt. Make sure it is straight.

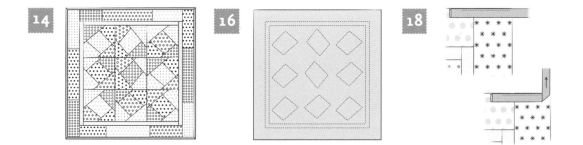

19. Holding the corner, fold the binding back down, south, aligning it with the raw edge. The folded corner must be square.

20. Pin and sew over the fold continuing down the next edge. Repeat with the other corners.

21. When you return to the starting point, turn under 1 cm of the beginning of the binding. Place the end of the binding into the fold, trim to size, then sew right over the top.

22. Fold the binding over to the back and pin along it: the corners will come together in neat mitres. Slipstitch into place.

TOP TIPS

- Patchwork shops sell ready-cut 'fat quarters', which can be great time-savers.

- The crazy block left over from this quilt can be made into a matching cushion. Put a layer of wadding on the back, quilt it, then patch an 'envelope back' from other scraps (see technique, page 27).

Cross-stitch Cushion

I have to admit that I've always found cross-stitch slightly confusing. Which cross to start with? Where to go next? How to make sure your crosses all go the right way? Any time I've given it a go, I've always tied myself in knots and lost my patience. Then I met Emily Peacock.

Graphic designer Emily started out as a hobbyist cross-stitcher, and it was only when she combined her professional expertise with her crafting imagination that the cross-stitching world changed and she became its undisputed doyenne. Dismiss all thoughts of those old-fashioned samplers our grandmothers had on their bedroom walls. Thanks to Emily, cross-stitch has got funky. So be inspired and give it a go. As a former cross-stitch philistine, I swear that you'll be converted. The finished cushion measures approximately 39 x 29 cm.

YOU WILL NEED

- Appleton Brothers crewel wool
  3 skeins each of:
  Iron Grey 964
  Cornflower 461
  2 skeins each of:
  Scarlet 504
  Honeysuckle Yellow 693
  Kingfisher 482
  Heraldic Gold 844
  Iron Grey 968
  White 991
  Leaf Green 427
  1 skein each of:
  Brown Olive 313
  Scarlet 505
  Cornflower 464
  Peacock Blue 645
  Heraldic Gold 841
  Black 998

- Tapestry needle, size 20
- Zweigart 10 hpi mono
  interlock tapestry canvas
  60 x 45 cm
- Scissors
- Large sheet of paper
- Tracing paper
- Pencil
- String
- Tape measure
- Backing fabric and
  matching sewing thread
- Pins
- Sewing machine and zipper foot
  (optional)
- Sewing needle
- Polyester filling or cushion pad
  made-to-measure (see Top Tips)
- 40 cm closed-end zip
  (optional)

1. This design is made in counted cross-stitch, using two strands of crewel wool. The best method for using crewel wool is to cut a length and fold it in half. Thread your needle, keeping the looped end longer than the cut end. Come in through the back of your work, form half of your first cross-stitch and insert the needle through the loop to secure.
2. To finish a length of wool, run the needle through a few stitches at the back of your work, taking care not to run a dark colour behind a light colour. Go back a couple of stitches and run the needle through the back once more, in a loop-the-loop motion.
3. The chart opposite has been marked with arrows indicating the centre of the design. Fold your canvas in half and in half again to locate the centre point and position your design accordingly.
4. Begin stitching using the colour key given below the chart5
5. When you have completed the stitching, if your canvas is warped or creased, spray lightly with water on both sides, then carefully stretch and straighten it. Dry flat, then trim your stitched canvas so that there is a 2 cm border around it.
6. Take your large piece of paper and trace the outline of your stitched area onto it. Even up the edges of your tracing and cut around it – this will be the template for the back of your cushion.
7. Measure around your design (do this easily by running a piece of string around the outside, then measuring the string). Cut a strip of backing fabric to the thickness you would like your cushion to be, adding 4 cm for seams. Our cushion is 10 cm thick, so our strip was 14 cm wide.
8. With right sides together, fold the strip of fabric in half widthways and machine or back-stitch the short ends together with a 2 cm seam. Press the seam open. With right sides together, pin the circular strip to your stitched design. Machine or backstitch with a 2 cm seam. Clip the curves at the corners.

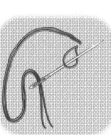

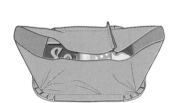

TOP TIPS

• Craft filling has a tendency to bunch up, causing an uneven finish, so if you are not using a made-to-measure cushion pad, Emily recommends buying good-quality cushion pads and cutting them open to use the superior filling inside them.

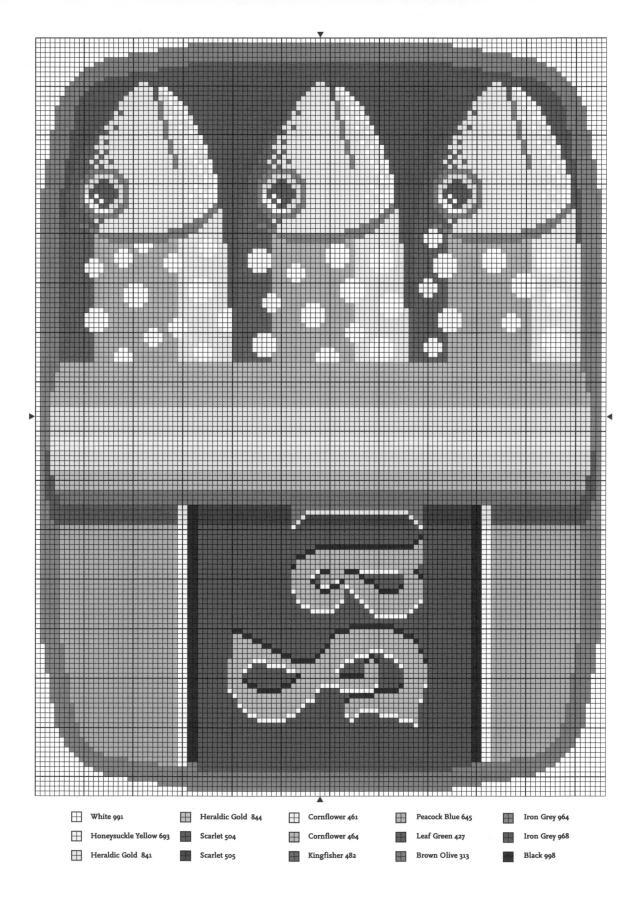

	White 991		Heraldic Gold 844		Cornflower 461		Peacock Blue 645		Iron Grey 964
	Honeysuckle Yellow 693		Scarlet 504		Cornflower 464		Leaf Green 427		Iron Grey 968
	Heraldic Gold 841		Scarlet 505		Kingfisher 482		Brown Olive 313		Black 998

1. Take your paper pattern and pin to your backing fabric. Cut around it, adding a 2 cm seam allowance all round.
2. With right sides together, pin this backing piece to the curved band running around your cushion. Stitch a 2 cm seam, leaving a gap of approximately 20 cm in the middle of one long side. Trim the seam allowances as necessary, being careful not to cut your stitching. Clip the curves at the corners.
3. Turn inside out and insert the polyester filling. Slip-stitch the gap closed.

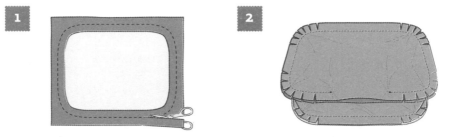

USING A CUSHION PAD AND ZIP

1. Take your paper pattern, fold in half lengthways and cut in half along the fold. Place the pieces on the straight grain of your backing fabric and cut them out, adding a 2 cm seam allowance around each piece.
2. Pin the pieces right sides together along one long side, making a 2 cm seam allowance. Machine or backstitch approximately 4 cm along the seam at either end. Using long stitches, tack along the opening on the same seam allowance. Press the seam open.
3. Lay your zip, with the tab and teeth face down, along the centre of your tacked seam. Tack in place. Using backstitch or a zipper foot on your sewing machine, stitch around the tape of the zip. Undo all the tacking.
4. With right sides together, pin this zippered backing piece to the curved band running around your cushion (see step 2 illustration above). Stitch a 2 cm seam. Trim the seam allowances as necessary, being careful not to cut your stitching. Turn inside out and insert the cushion pad.

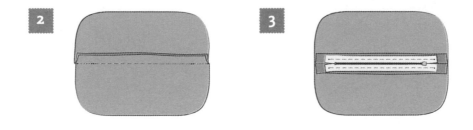

Textile Crafts

My love of fabrics and textiles is probably the worst-kept secret in the world. Like most crafters, I am a magpie and always on the lookout for material. At home I have baskets full of old tablecloths, napkins, handkerchiefs, remnants, even scraps and offcuts – nothing goes to waste. And because I've been collecting and hoarding over the years, I know that whenever creativity strikes and I want to start a new project, I'm bound to have a fabric in my collection to get me started.

I'm like a kid in a sweet shop when I go into antique and junk shops. It's guaranteed that I will leave with my purse a bit lighter and my fabric collection a bit bigger. And it really doesn't matter whether I have a crafting project in mind for my finds; if I like something, I buy it and worry later about how I'm going to use it. If you know where to look, you'll find old curtains, sheets, blankets, table linen … the list is endless, but remember, you can't go into these treasure troves with a shopping list because you never know what you're going to find. My advice is to pop in as often as you can to catch the best bargains and the most interesting finds. And make sure you check the fabric thoroughly – the last thing you want is to take home a beautiful piece, only to find a big hole in one corner, or to unleash a moth infestation in your cupboard.

My motto when searching for a house is to make friends with the agent, and I recommend you do the same with your local antique seller. That way, if they know you have a passion for textiles and are on the lookout for something in particular, they will keep it and let you have first dibs. Visiting antiques fairs and markets requires the same approach: get there early to bag the best bargains, and make friends with the sellers (chances are they are regulars and you will bump into them again on the circuit). The more you go to these places, the more you will get to know what is

available and what price you should be paying. Practice makes perfect (well, that's my excuse for buying), and buying second-hand is definitely a cheap way of sourcing fabrics for your projects.

Collecting textiles is recycling at its best, and virtually any fabric can be turned into something new, so think twice before getting rid of that old woolly jumper or dated silk blouse from the back of your wardrobe. Ask your family and friends to give you first look when they are having a clear-out of their wardrobe and cupboards. As the saying goes, one man's trash is another man's treasure.

My final piece of advice is to become familiar with the different types of textile available. Once you understand fabric, you will know what you might be able to make from it. For example, fabrics with a strong, firm weave are great for soft furnishings and upholstery, whereas nice soft cotton is perfect for making a quilt for your bed.

Of course, there are also amazing fabric designers all around Britain who are producing beautiful and original textile designs. The craftsmanship that goes into these fabrics means they're often pretty pricey, especially if you want to make large items, such as curtains. It's always worth checking out designers' websites and fabric shops as they often sell off remnants of top-quality stuff cheaply, so you can still get a fabulous fabric for a bargain price. This might mean you don't get your first choice and that you have to be more creative with your project, but we all love a crafting challenge, don't we? Remember, you don't have to fill your home with brand new materials. My solution is to mix and match old and new, and I think Meadowgate is a stylish example of this.

I feel very strongly that we should be supporting our British craftsmen and women because we have an extraordinary heritage. Weaving was a thriving cottage industry in sheep-farming areas in the eighteenth century, but it was during the Industrial Revolution of the nineteenth century that the fortunes of British textiles turned around and really put their mark on the global stage. With the invention of some innovative machines, mass-production began and textile mills sprang up all over the north of England, most notably in Manchester and Lancashire. Today Britain remains a leading

centre for textiles, with the industry producing around £8.5 billion worth of them every year. Let's continue to support this traditional industry – it's all about supply and demand, so the more we buy British, the more we will produce.

Now comes the most important question: what do you do with all the textiles that you have found and stashed away? This chapter is full of great ideas.

I've always loved the alchemy involved in transforming fabric using dyes, and I suspect early humans enjoyed it too. Archaeologists have dated some examples of plant-dyed materials to the Neolithic period, over 10,000 years ago. But with the invention of chemical dyes in the nineteenth century, the use of natural dyes fell out of favour. Luckily, at the same time as the Industrial Revolution was taking over production, the Arts and Crafts movement was working hard to keep alive traditions that would otherwise have been lost. William Morris, one of the figureheads of the movement, made extensive experiments with natural dyes, and, in collaboration with textile entrepreneur Thomas Wardle, created colours of a quality that exceeded any chemical dyes available at the time. Inspired by this, I asked dyeing expert Helen Melvin to share her method for dyeing fleece, and all is revealed on page 67.

Trumping this ancient craft is felting, using the oldest textile known to man. Felting is the process of tangling fibres, and, like most things, came about by accident. Legend has it that a man walking across the desert stuffed a handful of sheep wool or camel hair into his shoes to stop them rubbing. The friction from walking and the moist warmth of his feet turned the wool into felt. Whether or not this is true is a matter of debate, but it's a great story and felt is certainly a fun fabric to craft with. I recommend you start with the lovely felt heart decoration on page 65.

Another fun thing to do is needlefelting, which involves using a special tool to tangle fibres together in the design of your choice. It began life as an industrial process to combine synthetic and plant fibres in textiles. However, in the 1980s a husband and wife team developed needlefelting as a handicraft, and I for one am so glad they did. I made the prettiest little robin for my entry into the New Forest County Show, and can categorically say that needlefelting is one of my all-time favourite crafts. You don't

need any great skill to do it, and all mistakes can be easily corrected, which is brilliant for those who, like me, aren't always as neat and tidy as they'd like to be, and also love breaking the rules occasionally. See page 61 to make your own robin.

One of my best fabric-crafting experiences ever was in Devon at Clovelly Silk, where I was shown how to transform a length of velvet into a devoré scarf. The process, developed in France during the seventeenth century as a way of producing poor man's lace, was the brainchild of Joseph Jacquard, the man who invented a mechanised loom for making complex textiles such as brocade. Watching the devoré paste devour the fibres of the velvet to leave a pattern behind is spellbinding, and I would highly recommend giving it a go (see page 57).

With so many crafts to choose from, I hope you will find at least one that piques your interest, and enjoy taking a textile and turning it into something useful or beautiful. This really is one of the most satisfying things you can do.

Devoré Silk Scarf

I passionately believe that we should all be supporting local British businesses as much as we can. Near Meadowgate is Clovelly Silk, a family business run by Ann Jarvis and her daughter Ellie, which specialises in screen-printing designs onto silk. They taught me the devoré process, which uses an acidic paste to devour areas of velvet pile to leave behind a beautiful design. It's much easier than you might think and even the simplest design produces a stunning effect.

YOU WILL NEED

- Paper and pencil
- Plain paper for template (same size as your silk screen because you want the paste to go through your cut-out areas, not to escape around the edges)
- Scissors
- Old sheet
- 1 scarf-sized length of silk/viscose velvet
- Masking tape
- Silk screen (suitable size for your design)
- Latex gloves
- Devoré paste
- Squeegee (to fit inside your silk screen)
- Paintbrush(es)
- Hairdryer

1. Start by drawing a simple design, such as butterflies or leaves, on your paper. Cut around the shapes, then arrange them on your plain paper and draw around them. Cut out the shapes and your stencil is ready.
2. Cover a table or flat surface large enough for your scarf with a couple of layers of old fabric or sheets, firmly fixed, to provide a soft, flat surface.
3. Place your fabric, pile-side down, on the table and tape it around the edges to hold it steady.
4. Position your stencil on the fabric where you want to print your design. Place your silk screen over the stencil.
5. Now you're going to add the devoré paste, so put on some latex gloves. Place the squeegee close to one end of the frame and pour some devoré paste along the narrow space between it and the frame. Use the squeegee to firmly 'pull' the paste across the screen. Repeat the pulling six times.

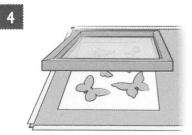

6. Gently lift the screen, peeling it back from one side. Your stencil should now have stuck to the screen.
7. Repeat steps 4 and 5 down the length of the scarf, repositioning the screen where you want the pattern.
8. Using a hairdryer, and without moving the fabric, dry the stencilled areas.
9. Once completely dry, press with a hot, dry iron – do not use steam. The printed area will burn (like toast) as you iron, but this is normal, so don't be alarmed.
10. Once thoroughly ironed, use your fingers to rub away the burnt fibres, taking care not to breathe in the dust.
11. When all the devoured areas have been removed, wash the velvet using a gentle soap. Rinse thoroughly and dye it if you like. Allow to dry, then iron again and your devoré silk scarf is now ready.

TOP TIPS

- Devoré fabrics dye beautifully using cold-water dyes. The natural and synthetic fibres in viscose velvet take the dye differently, creating a subtle kind of two-tone effect.

- To add further interest to your design, use a brush to dribble or paint devoré paste onto your fabric.

❧ Needlefelt Robin ❧

My first lesson with textile designer and needlefelter extraordinaire Jayne Emerson was so-o-o much fun. There are several types of needlefelting, but the one shown here involves using a special mat that resembles an upturned brush, and a spring-loaded punch that encloses special barbed needles. In this project you put fleece over a felt design and stamp the tool up and down to entangle the fibres and create a 3D image. It produces fantastic results really quickly – a bit like fuzzy felts for grown-ups.

YOU WILL NEED

· ·

- Tailor's chalk pencil
- Sheet of brown felt
- Scissors
- Scrap of black felt
- Clover mat and tool

- Woollen fleece in brown, red, white and grey
- Feather
- 2 beads, for eyes
- Needle and thread

- Long skewer
- Brown florist's tape
- Glue (optional)

1. Using the tailor's chalk, draw two bird shapes and two wings, as seen below, onto the brown felt. Cut out the shapes.
2. Cut a small triangular shape for the beak from the scrap of black felt and set aside.
3. Put one of the body shapes on the Clover mat. Take a small tuft of brown fleece and lay it on the felt, then begin lightly punching the Clover tool up and down (watch your fingers as the needles are very sharp). It doesn't matter if your fleece spills over the edges: if you stamp lightly, you can easily rectify mistakes, and you can also trim the bird later. Keep lifting the robin up to avoid needlefelting it to the mat. Continue adding fleece to the bird in the appropriate colours (see opposite) – rather like painting with fleece.

4. Once you are happy with your design, repeat it on the other bird shape (just remember the two sides should be facing opposite directions so that they match up when put together).
5. Repeat the needlefelting process with the wings.
6. Now needlefelt a wing to each robin shape; you will only need to punch at the base of the wing to give a 3D effect.
7. Place the two sides of the bird together, insert the beak and punch around the edges to secure. You will need to hold the wings out of the way, and you should also leave a small gap under the bird towards the tail end.
8. Stuff the robin lightly with a small amount of brown fleece, add the tail feather, then seal the gap with the Clover tool. (You might want to trim your feather into proportion with your robin, but I love the unrealistic flamboyance of mine.)
9. Stitch two beads onto the face for the eyes.
10. Wrap the skewer in the florist's tape. Make a small hole on the underside of the bird by delicately pulling the two sides apart, and insert the sharp end of the skewer. Add a little glue if necessary, or take a single needle from the Clover tool and use to felt the skewer in place.

TOP TIPS

- Wool works best for needlefelting as the fibres have scales that interlock easily, making the felting permanent.

- Try to keep your felting tool at 90 degrees to the cloth to avoid bending or breaking the needles.

- If you want to do fine detail, remove one needle from the tool and use it by hand. Take care when doing this because the needles are very sharp and rather brittle.

- To get rid of any visible punched holes in the finished piece, run a needle over the surface to gently move the fibres.

❦ Felt Heart ❧

Working with felt is an absolute joy, and this beautiful heart decoration is simple and effective. It's a lovely way of sprucing up any room in the house, and creates a cosy feeling when hung over the handle of a door or cupboard. It's also a great gift to take when visiting a friend, and can be customised at Christmas to hang on the tree.

I learnt to make this heart when I visited Lapland, so it will forever remind me of coming in from the cold and getting snuggled up next to the fire. However, make it in different colours with flowery ribbons, and perhaps tuck some dried lavender inside, and it's a lovely reminder of warm summer days.

YOU WILL NEED

- Pencil
- Paper
- Scissors
- Pins
- Red felt fabric
- 1 x 50 cm length of 4 mm ribbon
- Needle
- Thread, either matching or contrasting
- Polyester stuffing or sheep fleece
- 2 small beads
- 2 small buttons

1. Draw a heart shape on paper and cut it out. Pin it to the felt and cut out two hearts.
2. Take the piece of ribbon and fold it in half. Place it down the centre of one heart so the loop sticks out at the top and the ends hang down below. Place the other heart on top and pin together.
3. Using a running stitch, sew around the heart about 5 mm from the edge, but leave a 2.5 cm opening.
4. Stuff the heart with fleece through the opening, then stitch closed.
5. Thread one or two beads onto the ribbon at the bottom of the heart, tying a knot to keep them in place.
6. Sew a button on both sides of the heart for decoration.

Madder   Rubia
          Tinctorium
Spindle Spun Welsh
           Fleece   2011

Persian Baries.
Rhamnus Catharticus
with Rusty Nails
Spindle Spun Welsh Fleece
by Helen Melvin

Weld + Ammonia
Reseda Luteola.
Spindle spun by
Helen Melvin   2011

❧ Natural Dyes ❧

Colour always puts a smile on my face, and I'm a firm believer that the world would be a happier place if we all injected a bit more colour into our lives. I was therefore thrilled to discover the work of Helen Melvin, an artist who specialises in making dyes from plants, bark and seeds, and uses them to dye natural fibres that she makes into the most beautiful landscapes. She's so passionate that she even has her own dye garden, which hosts around fifty-five plants that can be used for dyeing. Follow her instructions carefully and you'll soon be filling every day with colour.

HEALTH AND SAFETY NOTES

Dyeing is all about chemical reactions, so be sure to follow the instructions exactly for safe results.

- Always protect yourself with gloves and an apron, and make sure you cover surfaces with newspaper or plastic bin liners.
- Never use any receptacle for dyeing that you might want to use later for cooking.
- Do not eat or drink when using dyes or mordants (bonding chemicals).
- Keep dyes and mordants away from children and pets.
- Take care when using household ammonia: follow the instructions on the bottle and use in a well-ventilated area. Avoid the fumes and take special care if you wear contact lenses.

YOU WILL NEED

- Pure wool yarn, hand-spun or shop-bought
- Dyestuffs (see guide overleaf to select colours)
- Bucket or old washing-up bowl
- Washing-up liquid
- Several 500 ml jars
- Mordant – a chemical that bonds to both fibre and dye and acts as a bridge between the two; alum is the safest mordant, and can be poured down the drain after use
- Measuring spoons, from 1 tsp to 1 tbsp
- Large pan, to use as a water bath
- Bottle of household ammonia (optional)
- Weight (optional)

Note: Here we use the water bath method, which allows you to dye a variety of colours at one time without a huge amount of equipment. Ideally, this should be done over about three or four days to get the best results.

1. Weigh your yarn and make a note of the weight.
2. Using the table overleaf, choose your dyestuffs and work out how much you will need for your yarn.

. . . .

There are hundreds of plants that produce flowers in colours rich, vibrant or subtle, and many of these are suitable for making dyes. This table gives just a selection.

The rule of thumb is that for every 100 g of material (weighed clean and dry), you will need 100 g of dyestuff. The quantity of dyestuff required is given as a percentage. For example, 100% means that for every 100 g of yarn you need 100 g of dyestuff; 200% means that you need twice as much dyestuff to yarn (this is usually the case with dyes made from garden plants); as little as 25% or 50% may be needed of strong dyes such as logwood and madder.

DYESTUFF	PART USED	PREPARATION	WEIGHT OF DYE TO FIBRE OR YARN	SOAKING TIME	COLOUR AND SPECIAL NOTES
African marigolds (*Tagetes spp.*)	Flower heads	Whole	200%	None	**YELLOWS** Put a rusty nail in the jar for greens, and a teaspoon of ammonia at the end to brighten the colour.
Brazilwood (*Caesalpinia spp.*)	Bark	Chips	50%	24 hours	**REDS**
Tickseed (*Coreopsis spp.*)	Flower heads	Berries	100%	None	**YELLOWS** A teaspoon of ammonia at the end of the dyeing time will give a bright burnt orange.
Elderberry (*Sambucas nigra*)	Berries	Squashed	100%	24 hours	**PURPLE** Good strong colour at first, but fades in two years.
Hawthorn (*Crataegus spp.*)	Leaves	Ripped	200%	24 hours	**YELLOWS** Put a rusty nail in the jar for greens, and a teaspoon of ammonia at the end to brighten the colour.

DYESTUFF	PART USED	PREPARATION	WEIGHT OF DYE TO FIBRE OR YARN	SOAKING TIME	COLOUR AND SPECIAL NOTES
Logwood (*Haematoxylin campechianum*)	Bark	Chips	50%	None	**PURPLE** The chips may tangle with the fibres/yarns, so put them into a small muslin bag. A teaspoon of ammonia will change the purple to dark blue.
Madder (*Rubia tinctorum*)	Roots	Chopped or powdered	50%	24 hours	**REDS AND ORANGES** Prolonged heating will produce brown. Using the dye jar repeatedly will eventually give shades of peach, orange and coral.
Onion (*Allium cepa*)	Skin	Ripped	50%	24 hours	**TANS** Red onion skins give a redder colour than yellow onions.
Persian berries (*Rhamnus* spp.)	Berries	Whole	50%	24 hours	**YELLOWS** Put a rusty nail in the jar for soft olive green.
Walnut (*Juglans nigra*)	Nut and/or leaves	Soak nuts in water to soften; rip leaves	200%	24 hours	**BROWN/GREEN** Walnuts give a golden brown. The leaves produce a yellow-green.
Weld (*Reseda luteola*)	Leaves, small stalks and seed heads	Chopped	200%	24 hours	ACID YELLOW Pour hot water over the chopped plant material. At the end of the dyeing time add a teaspoon of ammonia to give a fluorescent yellow.
Rhubarb (*Rheum* spp.)	Root	Chopped	100%	24 hours	**MUSTARD YELLOW** At the end of the dyeing time add a teaspoon of ammonia to change mustard yellow to dusty pink.
Yarrow (*Achillea* spp.)	Whole, including flowers	Chopped	100%	24 hours	**YELLOW** Very strong colour.

3. If using shop-bought yarn, fill a bucket with very hot water, add a tablespoon of washing-up liquid, then soak the yarn in it for 24 hours to remove any dressing (surface finish). Rinse in cold water and wring out by hand.

4. If using hand-spun yarn, 'wet out' the fibres by putting the yarn in a bucket and covering with cold water. You want the fibres to get really wet, so for best results leave for 24 hours.

5. While the yarn is soaking, put your chosen dyestuff into a 500 ml jar and fill it three-quarters full with water. Leave to soak for the time specified in the table on pages 68–9.

6. To prepare the mordant take another 500 ml jar, half-fill with hot water and add 2 level teaspoons alum for every 100 g of yarn. Stir until it is completely dissolved, adding more hot water if necessary.

7. Fill a bucket three-quarters full with cold water. Add the dissolved alum and stir.

8. Add the wet yarn, which should be able to move freely, and leave for at least 12 hours.

9. Drain, rinse gently, then spin-dry in the washing machine.

10. Add the yarn to the jar of soaked dyestuff, then put the jar into the large pan. (You can do more than one dye at a time in the water bath – as many jars as will fit.) Add enough water to the pan to reach just under the rim of the jar(s).

11. Heat the pan slowly over a low heat for at least half a day. The water in the jars should be very hot but not boiling. After this time, switch off the heat and allow to cool.

12. If you want to modify the colour, add some ammonia (see table on pages 68–9). After adding it, put the lid on the dye jar immediately and leave closed until you can open it outdoors. This will allow the fumes to disperse safely.

13. Rinse the dyed yarn in an old washing-up bowl with cool water until the water runs clear, then give it a final hot, soapy rinse before hanging it out to dry under slight tension. The best way to do this is to hang the yarn on a washing line and attach a weight to the end of the fibres (Helen recommends using something like a small hammer). This means that your yarn will dry straight.

TOP TIPS

• The dyes in the jars will get paler with each use, so use them several times to achieve paler shades. If you don't want to use them straight away, put a lid on the jar. You might be surprised by the colour that develops.

• Natural dyes can also be used with patchwork pieces, knitted squares or lengths of silk.

• Many companies sell natural dyes. See page 220 for suppliers.

Paper Crafts

The term 'paper craft' encompasses a wide variety of techniques – far more than I ever believed possible, and certainly far beyond anything I had previously attempted. I was, and remain, astonished at the beautiful things you can make from paper.

Paper-making itself is one of the earliest crafts, dating back to around AD 105, when a Chinese courtier presented the first sheets of paper to the emperor. From China it quickly spread around the world, and once industrialisation hit, there was no holding it back. By the nineteenth century it had become an inexpensive everyday item and brought about a huge culture shift by bringing information to the masses. Paper literally changed the world.

These days paper is something we take for granted – in newspapers, food packaging, giftwrap, books … You can't get through a day without coming across it in some shape or form, and when you start to explore what can be done with it, I think it will wow you just as it did me.

Paper craft is one of the most accessible crafts out there, and one of the cheapest. You can buy paper just about anywhere on the high street. Children's toy shops are packed to the rafters with lovely paper craft supplies, and they can even be found in big supermarkets, so you can pop them into your trolley while doing the weekly shop. It's guaranteed there'll be no costly mistakes, and if anything goes wrong, you can just start again. What could be better? Even the most sceptical of potential crafters can't argue with that, so let's get the next generation of craft designers and makers started early and feed their imaginations.

I've said it before and I'll say it again: when you get going in crafts, the best thing you can do is collect, collect, collect. Paper is everywhere, so you've got no excuse not to have a box full of the stuff ready for crafting. Paper and embellishments can be bought from crafting shops and online, and paper craft magazines often have free gifts. However, if you start looking, all these things are freely available almost everywhere. Reuse bits of cards that people have given you, or remove bows and ribbon from chocolate boxes to glue onto your creations. Search junk shops for old beads to attach to paper with wire. Look in charity shops for clothes with lovely buttons that can be glued onto card. The possibilities are endless and inspiration can come from anywhere – even plain old brown paper or newspaper can be transformed into something wonderful. Armed with these items, plus a pair of scissors and some glue, you'll be off.

One of the best places to start in the paper-crafting world is with a greeting card (see page 97). Written greetings go way back to the ancient Chinese and Egyptians, but it was the introduction of the postage stamp in 1840 that increased the greeting card's popularity in Britain. What was previously an expensive, personally delivered item became an affordable means of personal communication. I absolutely love it when someone gives me a homemade card because it shows they've put thought and care into the occasion. I remember making Mother's Day cards as a child and seeing the joy on my mum's face when she opened them. Receiving my first one made by my son at nursery was equally special, and much more personal than any present he (or his father) could have bought. The next time you're heading towards the card shop, turn around and give the homemade alternative a try yourself.

If you want to build on the skills you've acquired in making cards, try out the family scrapbook project (see page 103), which takes card-making techniques to a whole new level. Scrapbooking is another paper craft that goes way back, but it was in America during the 1980s that it hit the big time and took off in its current form. The trend then spread across the Atlantic to us in Britain, and huge numbers of people have taken it well and truly into their hearts. It's a fabulous way of preserving photos and memories, whether for yourself or someone else, and a great way of showing someone you care.

I'm also taking you right back to basics with a project to make your own paper (see page 99). It's the original, ancient craft and easy to do in your own home. Adding pretty dried flower petals and seeds from the garden, you can produce the most beautiful handmade paper, which can then be used for all sorts of things. It's so pretty and effective that it won't fail to impress.

From making paper it's just a short step to cutting it out, and there are two projects to show you how. The first one, a simple paper dolly chain (see page 87), is for children and a fun thing to make together. After that you can try the grown-up project, a delicate and beautiful paper bauble for the window (see page 93). Both these projects are fantastic ways to pass an afternoon and set the imagination racing.

Then there's papier mâché, a brilliant craft to do with your kids because it's messy, fun and gives quick results – perfect! This paper craft goes back almost as far as paper-making itself, to ancient China, where papier mâché was used to make warriors' helmets, which were then strengthened by layers of lacquer. It came to Britain in the 1670s, and in the mid-eighteenth century a man named Henry Clay found a way to make it as durable as wood. By the Victorian era, factories were churning out papier mâché items – everything from trays, snuffboxes and letter-holders to tables and chairs. This is all a far cry from the papier mâché I did at school, but it is a lovely craft to do at home, so why not try the snowman piñata on page 89? It's about the most fun you can have with a pile of old newspaper and some glue, and makes a lovely centrepiece for a winter party, so get the children involved and start the party with a bang.

Another project that uses up old newspaper is the brilliant bird sculpture on page 79. You create your basic shape out of scrunched-up newspaper and Sellotape, then decorate it by glueing pretty pieces of paper all over, a technique called découpage. What's great about paper sculpture and découpage is that you don't need any artistic ability to produce amazing results. In fact, I was so pleased with the little seaside bird I made that I entered it in the Royal Welsh Show découpage section.

One final word on paper crafts: there are no rights or wrongs, so you can't mess up. It's all open to your own artistic interpretation. If something doesn't turn out to your liking, simply put it in the recycling bin, pick up another piece of paper and start again. Brilliant!

Paper Sculpture Bird

Working with paper is fascinating because there are so many directions that you can take the craft in. Even newspaper can be transformed into the most amazing sculptures, as demonstrated to me by paper sculptor Jaina Minton. A former props maker, Jaina recycles the Sundays into 3D animals, then covers them with beautiful découpage paper. With a bit of imagination and creative thinking, you can sculpt almost anything, and it's something you and the kids will enjoy too.

YOU WILL NEED

- Newspaper
- Sellotape, in a dispenser
- Plastic-covered fencing wire, for the legs and feet
- Pliers
- Craft knife or scalpel
- Miniature screwdriver (optional)
- Glue gun
- Scissors
- Flexible card, for the beak
- 2 paintbrushes, one for painting, one for glueing
- PVA or découpage glue
- White acrylic paint
- Découpage paper (see Top Tips)
- Varnish

1. To make the body of the bird, scrunch up pieces of newspaper over and over again until soft, then squeeze together to form the required shape. (The more you scrunch and unscrunch the paper, the softer it gets and the easier it is to shape.) Sellotape over the paper to secure and smooth it as you go along.
2. When you are happy with the overall appearance of the bird, add a final layer of small pieces of Sellotape to make the bird form very tight and compact.
3. Now you have to make the bird's legs and feet. Take about 30 cm of wire and bend 10 cm of it at a right angle. At the base of that angle, bend the long part of the wire to make four toes in the shape of narrow petals.
4. Using pliers, twist each toe so it resembles a barleysugar stick with a loop at the end.

5. Spread out the toes so you have three at the front and one at the back. Repeat steps 3–5 to make another leg and foot in exactly the same way. Set aside.

6. Using the tip of a craft knife, prick two small holes in the base of the bird. Enlarge them slightly with a piece of wire or a miniature screwdriver, then insert the legs and stick them in place with a glue gun. Adjust the legs as necessary to make the bird stand securely.

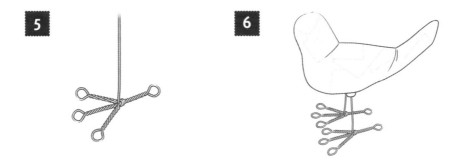

7. Cut out a cardboard triangle for the beak, curl it into a cone shape (it's easiest to do this around a pencil) and stick in place with Sellotape. Stuff a small piece of newspaper into the tip of the cone to make it solid.

8. Paint the bird with white acrylic paint and leave to dry. This gives a nice bright surface for the next step and will help the colours stand out.

9. While the bird is drying, cut your découpage paper into small squares or rectangles.

10. When the paint is completely dry, dilute some PVA glue with a little water and brush it onto the area you want to cover first. Add pieces of découpage paper one at a time, brushing the diluted glue over them as you go along. Make sure the papers overlap and are quite flat. Leave to dry.

11. Once fully dry, apply a layer of varnish to seal and add a glossy finish.

TOP TIPS

• Tissue paper works best for découpage as it is thin and moulds easily around curves and awkward shapes. You can buy this from stationery shops in a wide variety of colours. The Decoupatch brand, available from art shops, is made specifically for découpage. Although expensive, it is very nice to use and comes in lovely patterns. Other types of thin paper can work as well – anything between 40 and 60 gsm.

Paper Bead Necklace

It's amazing what you can do with paper. Who would have thought it could be used to produce lovely items of jewellery like the paper bead necklace opposite? Well, book sculptor and paper artist Phiona Richards did, for a start, and she showed me her clever but simple technique. You can use any paper you like – plain, patterned, old, new, thick, thin – whatever takes your fancy. Then you simply cut out circles, fold them in half, glue them together and thread them onto a cord. (Phiona also reveals how to make a slipknot fastening that costs nothing at all.) For a bit of extra interest, you can interweave the paper beads with any loose ceramic or wooden beads you happen to have in your jewellery box. The result is instant elegance for very little outlay. That's my kind of craft!

YOU WILL NEED

....

- Decorative paper or card, or pages from an old book
- Cutting mat
- Circle cutters (ours were 4 cm and 3 cm)
- Page from glossy magazine, as a glueing surface
- Glue stick
- Bulldog clips
- Leather or waxed cord, 100 cm long
- Coloured beads with a hole at least 3 mm wide

1. Place a sheet of your chosen paper on a cutting mat and use a circle cutter to cut out circles to the size(s) you want. The number you'll need per 'bead' depends on the thickness of your paper. For example:

   Book paper: cut 40 circles
   Decorative paper: cut 30 circles
   Wallpaper or thin card: cut 20 circles

2. To make a paper bead, fold each circle in half, making sure the edges meet neatly.

3. Take a page from a glossy magazine and fold along one straight edge so you have a flap about 4 cm deep. Place a folded circle on the page, tucking half of it under the flap.

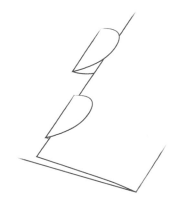

4. Spread glue on the exposed half of the circle. Place the glued side on top of another folded circle and peg together using a bulldog clip. Repeat this step until all your folded circles are glued together in pairs.

5. Using the same technique, glue the pairs together into sets of four folded circles. Continue doubling up until you have four segments.

6. Now glue your segments together to form a spherical bead. You might find three segments enough to make a full bead – the choice is yours. Note that each bead will naturally form a hole through the middle.

7. Repeat the previous steps to make two more beads.

8. Thread the cord with your paper beads, putting a coloured bead between them and at either end of the row.

9. The necklace is finished by creating an adjustable opening that incorporates two slip-knots. Start by placing the necklace on a flat surface. Take the left end of the cord and place it under the right cord.

10. Pass this same left cord over both cords.

11. Pass the left cord behind itself, through the loop and out to the right, going over itself again. Pulling on the left cord at both ends will tighten the knot. Try to get the knot as close as possible to the now short cut end of the cord or you will need to trim it later.

12. Turn the necklace over and repeat steps 9–11 to make a knot in the remaining loose end of cord. The knots can be slid along the cord to form an adjustable opening, and your necklace is now ready to wear.

TOP TIPS

- The generic name for all the bits and bobs needed in jewellery-making is 'findings'. Look this up online and you will see long lists of suppliers.

- Circle cutters come in a variety of sizes, so you can make beads in graduated sizes if you wish. The cutters are also useful for other paper crafts, such as card-making and scrapbooking.

- Stationers sell a huge range of decorative paper and card, so why not choose some to make jewellery that will match your outfit for a special occasion?

- Paper from old illustrated books makes distinctive and individual jewellery. You can buy old books for pennies at car boot sales or in charity shops.

Paper Dolly Chain

I absolutely love getting the kids involved in crafting, and this paper-cutting project by Mandy Shaw is a great place to start. You can use virtually any type of paper you have lying around the house, even newspaper produces a good effect (and the bonus is that you can teach the kids about recycling at the same time). Once you've cut the chains out, the kids can decorate them in any way they like. They look lovely strung across a window or from wall to wall indoors, and can look just as effective in the garden for summer parties.

YOU WILL NEED

- Large sheets of plain paper or newspaper
- Pencil
- Scissors
- Glue
- Paper doilies in 2 designs – we used red/white polka dots and plain gold (if you can find only white, get the kids to colour them)
- Coloured pens
- String (coloured if you like)
- Stapler
- Narrow ribbon, for hanging

1. Fold a piece of paper in half, and then in half again to create a concertina. Draw the outline of half a dolly and cut it out.
2. Repeat with a second piece of folded paper, then join the rows of dolls together with some glue. This will make eight dolls.
3. Fold a doily into eight (this means folding it in half three times). Cut along the fold lines to make eight triangular dresses. Snip off the pointed end and glue a dress to each dolly.
4. Take a different coloured doily and cut off the lacy border. Fold the border into eight equal pieces, then cut along the fold lines. Glue a piece to the back of each doll to create wings.
5. Using coloured pens, draw a face, hair and feet on each doll.
6. Make a small string bow and glue onto the front of each dolly's head.
7. Staple a length of ribbon to each end of the dolly chain and hang up.

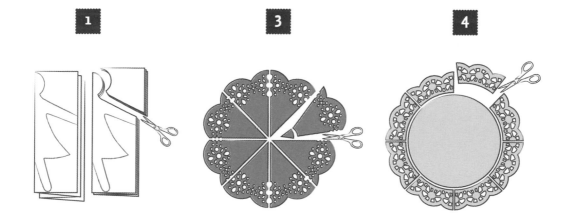

⁓⁓ Snowman Piñata ⁓⁓

It's not often something is made to be deliberately broken, but that's the case with our piñata, designed by Mandy Shaw. The idea of beating a container to release sweets and money began in Spain, but is now popular at children's parties around the world.

The original object started life as a clay pot decorated with colourful paper before it evolved into the papier-mâché form we know today. In fact, the word *piñata* means 'joined or bound in a bundle', a good description of the finished object, which can be made in any shape you want. Simply follow the instructions below, then hang it from the ceiling or, even better, out in the garden, and let the kids go at it in turn with a large stick until the goodies inside escape. What fun!

YOU WILL NEED

- Papier-mâché paste (1 cup flour to 2 cups water)
- Several sheets of newspaper
- Several sheets of white paper
- 2 balloons (1 large for the body, 1 small for the head)
- 2 bowls to sit the balloons in
- Vaseline
- Scissors
- Goodies for inside the piñata: sweets, trinkets, glitter, etc., plus tissue paper
- String
- Masking tape
- 8 buttons, for the eyes, mouth and body
- Crêpe paper in 3 or 4 different colours

1. Make a quantity of papier-mâché paste.
2. Tear the newspaper and white paper into strips 5 cm wide, keeping the white paper in a separate pile.
3. Blow up the balloons. Sit them each in a bowl to hold them steady while you work on them.
4. Lightly smear Vaseline all over the balloons (this makes them easier to remove later).
5. Dip a strip of newspaper in the paste and stick it to a balloon. Continue doing this until both balloons are covered, then leave to dry for at least 3 hours.
6. When they are fully dry, cover again with another layer of paste-soaked newspaper and leave to dry for 3 hours. Once dry, cover with a layer of white paper strips.
7. Once all the layers are completely dry, pop both the balloons and pull them out.
8. Cut around the hole left in the bigger balloon (the body) to make it about 7.5 cm in diameter. Fill with sweets, glitter, treats and tissue paper.
9. Pierce a hole on either side of the snowman's body, thread a long piece of string through them and knot the ends together. This loop will be used to hang up the finished piñata. Stick some masking tape around the holes for added strength.
10. Attach the smaller balloon (the head) to the body with masking tape. Paste another layer of white paper strips over the tape to hide it. Leave to dry for 3 hours.
11. Once it's ready, decorate the snowman: use buttons for the eyes and mouth, a wad of crêpe paper for his nose. Stick one or more buttons on his body, and make a hat and scarf out of more crêpe paper.
12. Hang up the piñata, ready for the party to begin.

Paper Bauble

Although paper-cutting is an ancient craft, it readily lends itself to modern interpretations, as shown here by the designer Sarah Morpeth. Her beautiful paper bauble is inexpensive and surprisingly quick and simple to make. In fact, it never ceases to amaze me that you can start with a blank piece of paper and end up with a work of art like this. You've just got to try it.

YOU WILL NEED

- Tracing paper
- Pencil
- 1 sheet A4 cartridge paper, about 160 gsm (see Top Tips overleaf)
- Cutting mat or a really thick piece of cardboard
- Craft knife or scalpel (Sarah uses a Swann Morton handle and no. 10A blades, but whatever you use, be sure to change the blade as soon as it gets blunt – see Top Tips overleaf)
- Crochet cotton or embroidery silk (for hanging the bauble)

1. Photocopy the design overleaf to whatever size you want, then trace around it and transfer to your sheet of cartridge paper.
2. Place the paper on your cutting mat. Starting in the middle of the design, cut along the black lines with your craft knife. Avoid twisting and turning the knife blade – turn the paper instead. And rather than trying to cut curves in one long line, make several small cuts – it doesn't matter if you cut the waste areas into lots of little pieces.
3. When you have finished cutting out the inner part of the design, cut around the outer circle, remembering the cutting tips in step 2.
4. Thread a length of crochet cotton or embroidery silk through the hole at the top of the bauble and tie the ends together. Try hanging the decoration in a window or in front of a mirror. You could also try varying the size of the decoration, making it from coloured paper, and hanging several together in a group.

—— CUTTING LINE   ▢ WASTE AREA (CUT THIS PART AWAY)

TOP TIPS

• Choose the right weight of paper for your project. This is usually quoted in grams per square metre (gsm). Standard paper for photocopying is around 80 or 90 gsm, while good-quality greetings cards often use card of 200–220 gsm. It's worth experimenting to see how cutting various weights of paper differs. Sarah normally uses cartridge (sketchbook) paper of around 160 gsm for her projects as it's sturdy and durable.

• If you are going to do a lot of paper-cutting, it is worth investing in a cutting mat. They have a bit of 'give' in them and provide a firm, steady base for cutting into.

• Always use a really sharp, new blade and change it frequently. You should hardly have to apply any pressure – a light stroke will cut the paper.

❧ Greeting Card ❧

We British love our cards. A staggering 2.2 billion cards a year pass through our hands, and it costs us around £1.07 billion. That's a lot of cash, so I say let's save ourselves some dosh by making our own. The gorgeous embossed card shown here, designed by Cheryl Owen, is full of beautiful detail and won't fail to impress.

YOU WILL NEED

- 1 ready-made blank card, folded size about 19 x 12.5 cm
- Scrap paper
- Floral rubber stamps – ours were 10 x 7.5 cm and 6.5 x 6.5 cm
- Ink pads – we used light green and lime green
- Piece of white card, about the size of your folded card
- Clear embossing powder
- Heat gun (optional)
- Craft knife
- Metal ruler
- Piece of lime green card, 6.5 cm square
- Spray adhesive
- Adhesive foam pads

1. Lay your folded card right side up on a sheet of scrap paper. Press the larger rubber stamp onto the light green ink pad, making sure the whole surface of the stamp is inked. Press the stamp firmly onto the front of the card, then lift smoothly away. Repeat the stamping randomly to the front of the card to create a background design, and allow the stamp to extend onto the scrap paper so that all areas of the card are covered. Leave to dry.
2. Press the smaller rubber stamp onto the lime green ink pad, again making sure the whole surface is evenly inked. Press the stamp firmly onto your piece of white card, then lift smoothly away. Pour embossing powder onto the stamped flower. Tip the excess powder onto scrap paper.
3. Light a hob on your cooker and hold the stamped flower face up about 10 cm above it until the embossing powder has melted. Alternatively, rest the stamped flower face up on a flat surface and hold a heat gun about 5 cm above it. Move the gun from side to side until the embossing powder has melted. It dries immediately.
4. With a craft knife and metal ruler, trim the white card to 6 cm square with the flower centred.
5. Using spray adhesive, stick the embossed flower centrally onto the lime green card. Place an adhesive foam pad (trimmed to size) at each corner on the back of the lime green card, then stick to the card with the stamped background 3 cm below the upper edge.

TO MAKE YOUR OWN BLANK CARDS

Take a rectangle of card (240 gsm is a good weight) and make a pencil mark at top and bottom where you want to fold it. Hold a metal ruler beside the marks, then run a bone folder (similar to a paper knife but made of bone) alongside the ruler to score a straight line. Now fold the card in half, keeping the scored line on the outside. Your card is now ready for decoration.

Handmade Paper

I always imagined that the process of making paper would be mysterious and difficult, not something you would tackle at home, but – as Cheryl Owen shows below – I was quite wrong. The only special equipment you need for this project is a deckle, a simple wooden frame with a muslin cloth stretched over it. This acts as a mould for the paper, and can be used time and time again.

As you'll see, with some simple ingredients and a tiny bit of patience, you really can produce the most beautiful paper speckled with seeds and petals – and use it in many different ways. Try it as wrapping paper for a present, a covering for a book, or use it with other paper crafts, such as greeting cards or scrapbooks (see pages 97 and 103).

YOU WILL NEED

- White cartridge paper: 2 sheets of A3 will make at least 8 sheets of 13 x 8 cm handmade paper
- 2 large bowls
- Flat-fronted wooden picture frame, 15 x 10 cm
- Rectangle of muslin or net curtain, 22 x 17 cm
- Staple gun
- Blender
- Dried seeds (lavender, fennel, etc.)
- Dried and pressed petals and leaves (roses, carnations, delphiniums, etc.)
- Flat synthetic sponge
- Tablespoon
- J-cloths

1. Tear the cartridge paper into pieces about 1.5 cm square. Place in a bowl and soak in water for at least 30 minutes.
2. Meanwhile, remove the glass and backing board from the picture frame and fold back the metal board supports. Place the frame face down in the middle of your muslin. Fold the fabric to the back of the frame and staple it smoothly and tautly in position.

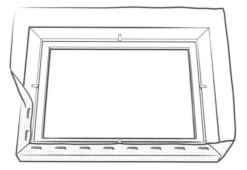

3. Half-fill a blender with the soaked paper. Pour in water until the blender is three-quarters full. Whizz the mixture to a pulp. You might need to do this in batches.

4. Tip the pulp into another large bowl. Add about 2 litres of water and stir well. With the wrong side of the deckle facing upwards, dip it into the bowl at an angle. Bring it level under the water, then slowly bring it out, allowing the water to drip through while you hold the deckle resting on the edge of the bowl.

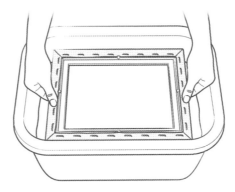

5. Sprinkle some dried seeds, petals and leaves at random on the pulp, or arrange them as you wish.
6. Using the sponge, gently press the pulp to squeeze out the excess water and keep the added materials in place. Spoon more pulp mixture over the added materials and again squeeze out the excess water by pressing the sponge all over the surface.
7. Lay a J-cloth flat on a work surface. Place the deckle wrong side down on one half of the cloth. Tap to release the paper onto the cloth, then remove the deckle. Fold the other half of the cloth over the paper to soak up the excess water. Open out the cloth again. Leave the paper to dry overnight.

TOP TIPS

- The size of paper made here is handy for craft projects. But if you want to produce larger sheets of paper, perhaps for wrapping, use a larger picture frame to make a bigger deckle.

- Cartridge paper is available in many different colours, so you don't have to work with white. Choose whatever colour you like and add petals as subtle or vibrant as you wish.

Family Scrapbook

Scrapbooking is currently one of the most popular crafts around, with thousands of dedicated followers. If you have never tried it, go online and you will find literally hundreds of websites dedicated to the craft, all brimming with ideas and supplies for creating your own. Now that I've had a go myself, I can understand why people get hooked. It's one of most therapeutic and satisfying crafts that I've come across because you really do have complete freedom to make it as simple or complicated as you like, and in the end you have a beautiful keepsake to treasure for years to come. Also, it can be done easily from your kitchen table without any expensive equipment.

While you can buy ready-to-fill albums from craft stores, this project, designed by Cheryl Owen, shows you how to make the album itself, and offers a design for a baby page to set things rolling. It's easy to follow and, I hope, will get your creative juices flowing to create a personal album that you or a loved one will treasure forever.

TO MAKE THE SCRAPBOOK
YOU WILL NEED

....

- 2 x A3 sheets card (500 gsm)
- Cutting mat
- Metal ruler
- Pencil
- Craft knife
- 2 x A3 sheets deep blue paper
- PVA glue with plastic spreader or a small piece of card
- 1 small sheet handmade paper (see page 99)
- 6 mother-of-pearl buttons, round and heart-shaped
- Large crewel embroidery needle
- White embroidery thread
- 2 x A4 sheets mottled blue paper
- Bone folder (optional)
- 20 x A4 sheets mottled blue card (240 gsm)
- Double-hole punch
- 4 x 6 mm metal eyelets and fixing tool
- 1 metre wire-edged pink/white ribbon, 5 cm wide

1. Place the card on a cutting mat and use a ruler and pencil to mark out two rectangles measuring 27 x 21.6 cm for the covers. Then mark out two strips measuring 21.6 x 2.8 cm for the hinges. Using a craft knife, cut out the shapes against a metal ruler. Set aside.

2. Now mark out and cut two rectangles of 34 x 25.6 cm on the deep blue paper.

3. Spread PVA glue thinly and evenly on one cover and hinge. Stick them 3 mm apart on the wrong side of one deep blue paper rectangle, with the paper extending evenly all around the card. Turn the paper over and smooth outwards from the centre to make sure the card is glued smoothly all over. Repeat to stick the other cover pieces. Leave to dry.

4. Snip the paper diagonally across each corner 6 mm from the card. Glue the diagonal edges of the paper over the corners of the card. Glue the straight edges of the paper over the edges of the card.

5. Place the small sheet of handmade paper on the front of one cover, which will be the front of your album. Position a button at one corner, with its holes just inside the edges of the handmade paper. Using a large crewel needle, pierce through the button-holes, then sew the button in place with white embroidery thread, tying the ends together on the underside of the front cover. Sew a button at the remaining corners in the same way, then sew one in the centre of each long edge of the handmade paper.

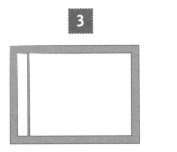
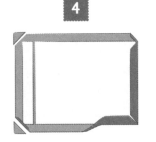
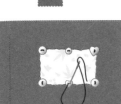

6. Spread PVA glue thinly and evenly on one sheet of mottled blue paper. Stick the paper centrally to the underside of one cover, covering the raw edges of the deep blue paper. Repeat with the remaining cover. Leave to dry.

7. Using a bone folder or the blunt edge of the craft knife, score across each mottled blue card 2.5 cm from the left-hand edge to form a hinge. Stack these pages a few at a time, then punch a pair of holes centrally in their hinges.

8. Place one page centrally on the wrong side of the front cover, matching the hinges. Using a pencil, mark the position of the punched holes on the front cover hinge. Resting it on a cutting mat, cut out the holes in the front cover with a craft knife, cutting through all the layers. Repeat on the back cover. Following the manufacturer's instructions, fix a metal eyelet through the album holes.

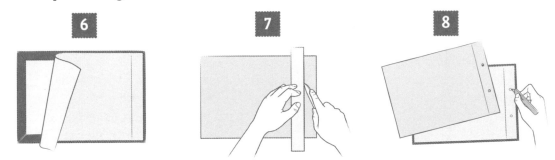

9. Stack the pages together between the covers. Thread the ribbon through the holes and tie the ends in a bow on the front. Trim the tails of the bow diagonally.

TO MAKE A BABY PAGE
YOU WILL NEED
....

- Pencil
- 3 sheets 13 x 8 cm hand-made paper, incorporating dried carnation petals (see page 99)
- Double-sided tape, 1.5 cm wide (see Top Tips)
- Ready-made tiny ribbon rose decoration

- All-purpose household glue
- Baby photograph
- Craft knife and metal ruler
- Cutting mat
- Coloured paper
- Spray adhesive
- Scissors
- 60 cm coloured satin ribbon, 1.5 cm wide

- 1 album page
- 20 cm gingham ribbon, 1 cm wide
- 2 flat-backed buttons
- Pair of baby socks
- Coloured embroidery thread and needle
- Curl of hair tied with thread

1. Draw the envelope templates below onto 2 sheets of handmade paper, making sure you match the upper edge of the front envelope to the deckle (rough) edge of the paper.

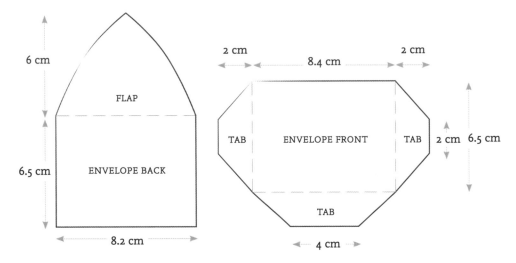

2. Place the back of the envelope on the front of the envelope with wrong sides together (i.e. the seeds and petals facing you). Fold the tabs along the broken lines and stick them to the back of the envelope with double-sided tape. Turn the envelope over, fold the flap down and stick the ribbon rose to it with household glue.
3. Trim the photo to size, cutting off the white edges, using a craft knife, a metal ruler and a cutting mat. Stick the photo to appropriate coloured paper with spray adhesive. Place on the cutting mat and cut a 3 mm border of the paper around the photo.
4. On a scrap of card, draw a triangle with a base of 3 cm and sides of 2.5 cm. Cut it out with a craft knife, then trace around it four times on leftover bits of handmade paper. Cut around the triangles with a craft knife, then cut a wavy slit in each mount (see opposite). Slip a mount onto each corner of the photograph.
5. Cut two lengths of satin ribbon 30 cm long. Fray one end of each length to a depth of 1 cm. Stick double-sided tape to the wrong side of the ribbon just inside the frayed end.

6. Lay the ribbons right side up on the album page 3.5 cm from the long upper and lower edges with one frayed end 2 cm from the right-hand edge of the page and the other frayed end 2 cm from the scored edge of the hinge. Carefully peel the backing paper off the tape to stick the ribbons in place. Trim the unfrayed ends of the ribbons level with the short sides of the page.

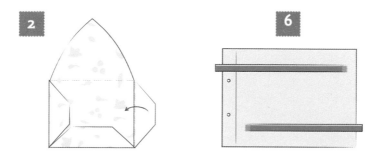

7. Cut a 20 cm length of gingham ribbon and tie in a bow. Trim the tails of the bow diagonally. Sew a button to each baby sock with coloured embroidery thread. Arrange the photograph, envelope, curl of hair and socks on the page, then stick in place with all-purpose glue. Apply the glue to the tied thread of the hair curl, then glue the gingham bow on top of it.

TOP TIPS

- Use acid-free archival double-sided tape to stick photos and decorative papers to the pages to ensure long-lasting scrapbooks.

- Store small treasures, such as letters and newspaper clippings, in little envelopes fixed to the page.

- A4 pages and 30 cm squares are the most convenient for albums because paper and card are readily available in these sizes.

Food Crafts

Food glorious food! As you might have gathered, I absolutely love to eat, so I adore the fact that my crafting journey has led me into the world of food. Combining my love of food with my passion for crafts seems like the perfect marriage. What could be better than eating what you've lovingly crafted? It's the ultimate reward for your hard work.

Recently, I've had the pleasure of meeting some fantastic crafts people making all kinds of food – jams, cheeses, cakes, ciders – you name it, it's out there. This area of the crafting world is huge and it's getting bigger all the time. In the late 1990s people grew sick and tired of mass-produced supermarket food, and created a demand for fresh, locally sourced produce. This led to the development of farmers' markets, and today it's estimated that there are 750 in the UK, which is great news for all of us – lovely local food and produce are now more readily available than ever. These markets attract farmers, of course, who sell their wonderfully tasty rare breed meat, sausages and pies, but alongside them stand dedicated local artisans, who set up stalls to sell an amazing range of breads, cheeses, preserves and much more. It's food straight from the fields, hedgerows and kitchens of local people. Combining the best local ingredients to give the best flavour, taste is the central quest of every single one of these producers.

Buying local means buying British, something I'm always banging on about, but it's so important to lend our support to British food crafters and artisans. Let's help them get stronger and stronger by buying from them whenever possible. You won't just be getting well-produced food – you'll be getting a flavour unique to the area. Take a look around and you'll find there are hundreds of local producers beavering away and creating amazing things from what is right on the doorstep. You can buy them from

your farmers' market, of course, but check the shelves of your local deli – it might stock something special and unique to where you live – and keep an eye out in the supermarkets because many have jumped on the bandwagon in the last few years. Get out there and tickle those taste buds.

Food might be fuel, but for me it's also one of life's greatest pleasures and my days seem to revolve around it. Eating out is fun, but for me, the best type of food is the homemade variety. In the days before mass production, artisan techniques were passed down from generation to generation and gave rise to family and regional specialities. Eating these delicious things has always been a huge joy, but it's not just the eating that's important: it's the love and care that goes into its creation. Making food is about putting your heart on your sleeve and giving part of yourself on the plate. When someone cooks for you, please remember not to judge their efforts too harshly – we all take criticism of our homemade food very personally.

Throughout history, food has always brought people together, from the earliest humans sharing their kill around the fire, to medieval peasants and monks eating bread and pease pottage, and royal courts tucking into feasts of roast venison. Food remains as important today as it was in the lives of our ancestors. For me, time spent eating with family and friends around the table is a great way of bonding and sharing, which is really what life's all about. The kitchen is the heart of the home – a cliché I know, but absolutely true. It's where we congregate as a family and chat about the day while eating our evening meal; where we sit around with friends and catch up on the news while enjoying lunch; and I find there is no bigger satisfaction in life than seeing the faces of my loved ones tucking into something I've spent time making myself. Nobody ever leaves my house hungry.

Home cooking is often a tradition passed down through families from generation to generation, so it's not unusual to find that the dishes we grew up with become our own staples too. It was my mother who taught me the basics of cooking, though it didn't happen in a formal way; instead I learnt from her as we went along. She taught me to make the perfect mashed potato, something that I still have a great passion for.

When we were growing up there were endless arguments in our house about whose turn it was to make the mash. I'm not necessarily the most adventurous cook, but, thanks to my mum, I'm good at the basic British staples, and in my view, that's a great start.

Over the years, I've picked up recipe ideas from here, there and everywhere. My recipe folder is packed with old family favourites, cuttings from magazines, and scraps of paper with recipes I've jotted down while visiting friends' houses. I've got to admit that I've not made every recipe in my bursting-at-the-seams folder, but the cuttings and scrappy notes provide inspiration when I'm stuck for what to make. Keeping a folder is something I would recommend you get into the habit of doing. As with all crafts, become a magpie and collect as many ideas as possible. You never know when you might get round to making an impressive salmon and watercress flan, or have an unexpectedly free afternoon to try your hand at a traditional brandy snaps.

One of my favourite meals ever is afternoon tea. It's widely considered that the ritual of taking afternoon tea originated with the Victorians, and in particular the Duchess of Bedford, who was Lady of the Bedchamber to the young Queen Victoria. The duchess started drinking tea with a small bite to eat in the mid-afternoon to keep her going until dinner, which was eaten around 7 p.m. This soon developed into a social occasion, and guests were invited to join the duchess for afternoon tea, which was served on the best china. It was a most elegant affair, and on offer were usually small sandwiches, with the crusts cut off, of course, and scones with jam.

Entering the afternoon tea competition at the Devon County Show gave me the opportunity to learn more about baking, and I'm thrilled to share what I learnt with you, including the most delicious scones and jam (pages 133 and 135). Despite scones being synonymous with Devonshire cream teas, Scotland lays claim to their invention, with the first print reference in 1513 from a Scottish poet. Originally made with oats, they are said to have been named after the Stone of Scone (or Destiny), upon which Scottish kings were crowned. Robert the Bruce and his warriors are reputed to have baked them on their shields and eaten them before going into battle. Whilst this may be the stuff of legend, the scone remains a filling and hearty addition to anyone's day.

If you want to continue your foray into baking, try the fruit cake recipe on page 115. We Brits have been making cakes like this ever since dried fruits first arrived here from the Mediterranean during the thirteenth century, but it was in the eighteenth century that they began taking a special place at celebrations, such as weddings. I am immensely proud of the fruit cake I entered into the Devon County Show. Inspired by a recipe the wonderful Rosie Davies taught me, I added my own twist and won first prize, which was absolutely thrilling. The icing on the cake was decorated with beautiful sugar flowers (see page 129), which are simple to make but so elegant.

While I'm by no means an expert cook or baker, I'm hoping that the crafts and recipes I'm passing on to you in this chapter will get your crafting juices flowing. For those who really can't bring themselves to turn the oven on, I've also taken a leaf out of Granny's book by showing you how to preserve fruit. No glut of produce need ever go to waste again, and making preserves means that you can enjoy the fruits of your labour all year round. You'll also be keeping up a tradition that started many centuries ago, when people first devised ways of storing provisions against the threats of famine, drought and warfare. Salting, drying and smoking were all popular, but the technique I show you on page 137 is pickling. Just try the blackberry vodka and you'll be converted to pickles forever.

The message I hope you'll get from this chapter is that food is fun. There are some yummy recipes with children in mind, and I guarantee they'll raise a smile with everyone. I've merely dipped my toe into what is a vast and exciting world, but once you've got the taste for food craft, you won't want to stop going back for seconds. And if it all goes wrong, simply scoff your mistakes and start again. Nobody need ever know …

Fruit Cake

'Cake' is a word that makes me happy. In whatever way, shape or form it comes, a cake brightens up my day, so I was really pleased when Rosie Davies taught me how to make this fantastic fruit cake and introduced me to a whole new world of baking. I always thought a fruit cake was for the more advanced baker, but this straightforward recipe is easy to follow and very forgiving of any minor mistakes. I even entered my own version of it, fully marzipanned and iced, for the cake competition at the Devon Craft Fair. Try it yourself as a last-minute Christmas cake, as a celebratory cake, or as a cake to have in the cupboard for when friends pop round. And the best bit? Licking the bowl clean once the cake is in the oven!

YOU WILL NEED

- 900 g of your favourite mixed dried fruit (dates, prunes, apricots, sultanas, currants, stem ginger), or you can use a packet of mixed dried fruit
- 300 ml dry cider
- 225 g butter
- 225 g soft brown sugar
- juice and finely grated rind of 1 lemon and 1 orange
- 1 tbsp black treacle (optional)
- 4 large eggs, beaten
- 225 g plain flour
- 1 tsp ground mixed spice
- ½ tsp ground nutmeg
- 170 g chopped mixed nuts (almonds, hazelnuts, pecans)
- about 20 whole almonds, to decorate the top
- about 6 tbsp apple brandy (ordinary brandy or whisky could be used instead)

1. Preheat the oven to 150°C/Gas mark 2.
2. Line a 20-cm cake tin with two layers of greaseproof paper. Make sure the paper around the sides goes about 5 cm above the rim of the tin so that none of the mixture escapes as it rises.
3. If your dried fruit is not prewashed, wash it all thoroughly, then chop up the larger pieces so they're about the size of the sultanas and currants.
4. Put all the fruit in a pan with the cider, bring to the boil and simmer for 2–3 minutes. Set aside and allow to get cold. The fruit should absorb all the liquid, but if there's any left, drain it off.
5. In a large mixing bowl, cream the butter and sugar with the finely grated rinds of the orange and lemon. Add the treacle, if using – it's great for flavour and colour, but if it's not to your taste, it can be left out (see Top Tips). Pour in the beaten eggs and mix well.
6. Sift the flour with the mixed spice and ground nutmeg and fold into the egg mixture.
7. Now stir in the soaked dried fruit, the chopped nuts and some of the citrus juices to produce a mixture that has a soft dropping consistency.
8. Spoon the mixture into the prepared tin, smooth the top, then make a shallow dent in the middle so that the cake will rise evenly as it cooks.
9. Arrange the whole almonds over the surface and add a sprinkling of brown sugar to give a lovely crunchy topping (don't add these things if you want to ice the cake).

10. Wrap a thick layer of brown paper or newspaper around the outside of the tin – as high as the lining paper – and secure with string. Place the tin on a baking tray lined with more brown paper and bake for 3 hours. Check the cake halfway through the baking time – if the top is getting too brown, cover it with a piece of brown paper.
11. Check the cake is cooked by inserting a skewer in the middle – it should come out clean. Remove the cake from the oven, prick it all over with a fine skewer and carefully pour the apple brandy into the holes. Allow the cake to cool completely before removing from the tin. To store, wrap in greaseproof paper and store in an airtight tin.

TOP TIPS

- Greasing the treacle spoon with a little vegetable oil will prevent the treacle from sticking to it.

- Tying brown paper around the outside of the tin helps the cake from cooking too fast and burning.

- This cake can be marzipanned and iced as soon as it's cold, but if you plan to do that, don't add the almonds or sugar on top.

Ice-cream Balls

As you probably already know, any craft that involves edible glitter is a winner with me, so these ice-cream balls, devised by Louisa Carter, hit the jackpot. Once you get the hang of the method, you can be creative and customise the balls with different flavours of ice cream or your favourite type of chocolate, and everyone can choose their own toppings.

YOU WILL NEED

- 1 large tub of ice cream (whatever flavour you like)
- 1 large bar of chocolate (white, milk or dark)
- Range of toppings – desiccated coconut, edible glitter, crushed pistachios, mini-chocolate chips, hundreds and thousands, or whatever else you can think of

1. Line a baking tray or large platter with greaseproof paper. Lay out all your equipment and ingredients before you start as you've got to work quickly.
2. Using a melon baller dipped in a glass of hot water, scoop out as many balls of ice cream as will fit on the tray. Place in the freezer and leave until they are frozen solid.
3. When the ice cream is frozen, melt the chocolate in a heatproof bowl set over a pan of simmering water.
4. Meanwhile, put each of your toppings on small plates ready for the dipping.
5. When the chocolate has melted, take the tray of ice-cream balls out of the freezer. Using two forks, pick up one of the balls and dip it into the chocolate, making sure you cover it completely. Dip it immediately into your chosen topping and roll around until it is fully covered. Place back on the baking tray. Repeat with all the other balls, then return them to the freezer until you are ready to serve.

Party Jelly

Imagine my delight when I met Sam Bompas of Bompas & Parr, a company that has turned jelly-making into an art form. Sam taught me the basics of making fresh fruit jelly at home without a jelly cube in sight, and since then I've embraced his way of making this quivering treat, much to the delight of my kids. This recipe requires a 500-ml jelly mould. If your granny doesn't have one lurking in her kitchen, you can do what I did and use a child's sandcastle bucket – thoroughly scrubbed of course.

YOU WILL NEED

- 1 kg plums (or virtually any fruit you have to hand)
- About 120 g sugar
- Juice of ½ a lemon
- 5 sheets gelatine (platinum grade is the highest quality, and available from most supermarkets)
- Small sweets or chunks of fresh fruit (optional)

1. Put the plums in a saucepan with a small amount of water and sprinkle with 20 g sugar. Cover and simmer on the hob until the fruit is soft and mushy.
2. Put a muslin cloth over a sieve and place over a measuring jug. Pour the mushy plums into the cloth and leave to drip until you have 300 ml juice in the jug. This can take a while, so be patient. Don't force the juice through or it will become cloudy.
3. In a saucepan, dissolve 100 g of the remaining sugar in 100 ml water to make a sugar solution. Pour into the plum juice, add another 100 ml water and the lemon juice and mix together in the jug.
4. Put the gelatine and a little of the plum liquid in a heatproof bowl and set over a saucepan of boiling water (the bowl should not touch the water). Heat, stirring, until the gelatine has dissolved – about 2 minutes.
5. Sieve the gelatine mixture back into the jug of juice and stir thoroughly.
6. Pour half the mixture into your mould. If you want to add sweets or chunks of fresh fruit, put them in at this stage, then top up mould with the rest of the mixture. Place in the fridge for 6 hours.
7. When the jelly is set, dip the mould in hot water for 10 seconds to release the jelly, then invert onto a plate to serve.

TOP TIPS

- You need 100 ml liquid per sheet of gelatine: too much and your jelly will collapse; too little and it will be bouncing off the walls.

- To make an adult version of the jelly, use 100 ml of any alcohol you like (e.g. port, brandy, wine) instead of the water that is added with the lemon juice.

- Don't waste the fruit pulp left in the muslin: you can serve it as a compote with yoghurt or cream, or use it as the basis of a fruit mousse.

Marzipan Penguins

Quick and easy to make, these marzipan penguins, created by Louisa Carter, add a special touch to any party or gathering, and believe me, they are guaranteed to impress even the smallest and pickiest of guests. If you want to give it a go, you can make the marzipan yourself really easily, but if you're a busy working mum like me, there's no shame in going for the ready-made stuff – both work just as well.

YOU WILL NEED

- Marzipan
- Food colouring in black and orange
- Small paintbrush

1. Take a chunk of the marzipan, large enough for one penguin (you can make them any size you like) and gently knead to soften it up. Cut off a chunk and roll into a ball to make the body.
2. Next, take two smaller pieces of marzipan and roll into two small balls for the eyes.
3. Take another chunk (enough for the head, wings and feet) and add a few drops of black food colouring. Knead until the colouring is evenly spread through the marzipan, then roll out a ball for the head and two smaller balls for the feet. Attach these to the body by pressing them into place.
4. Now make two oval discs for the wings, making one end wider than the other. Attach the wider end to the side of the body, just below the head. Flick up the narrow end.
5. Attach the eyes to the head, then dip the paintbrush in the black colouring and put a small dot in the middle of each eye.
6. Take the last piece of marzipan and roll into a small cone for the beak. Press this onto the face. Clean your paintbrush and paint the beak orange.

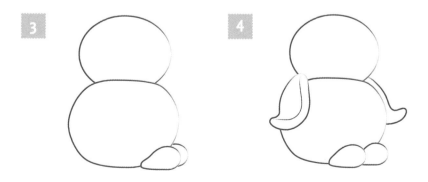

Banana Cake

Baking is fantastic fun. Combining all those ingredients, watching through the oven door and then finally tasting the end result – what could be better! I also love the exactness of baking. Making sure you follow the recipe to the letter, appeals to my neat and tidy side and gives me a great sense of satisfaction.

Everyone has a failsafe recipe that they swear by, and for years mine has been this banana cake. I know that I can whip it up in minutes and it will come out looking great and tasting even better. Add it to your list of tasty, easy bakes and know you will be guaranteed success.

YOU WILL NEED

- 4 ripe bananas
- 150 g melted butter
- 2 eggs
- 175 g plain flour
- 2 tsp baking powder
- 1 tsp bicarbonate of soda
- Pinch of salt
- 1 tsp vanilla

1. Preheat the oven to 180°C/Gas mark 4. Line a 21 x 11 cm loaf tin with greaseproof paper.
2. Mash up the bananas in a large bowl, then mix in the butter and eggs. Add the rest of the ingredients and mix well.
3. Pour the mixture into the prepared tin and place in the oven for about 45 minutes. The cake is ready when a skewer stuck into the middle comes out clean.

Sugar Flowers

One of the things I love most about crafts is the part (usually at the end) when you get to make everything look pretty. Victoria Cranfield taught me how to make these really quick and simple sugar flowers, and they really do add the perfect finishing touch to the top of any cake or pudding. I put them on top of my fruit cake (see page 117) at the Devon County Show and, much to my surprise, did rather well in the single cake competition. I hope it was due to the quality of my cake, but I'd also like to think that the flower decorations went a good way to helping my entry to stand out.

YOU WILL NEED

- 1 egg white
- Edible flowers, such as primroses, pansies, rose petals, thyme flowers, purple verbena
- Lemon verbena leaves
- Bowl of caster sugar

1. Put the egg white in a bowl, add ¼ teaspoon cold water, then beat for 2–3 seconds, until there are a few bubbles.
2. Dip a soft paintbrush in the egg mixture and brush it over your flowers and leaves. They need only a very light coating.
3. Dip each coated flower or leaf into the sugar, making sure it is evenly covered, then shake off the excess.
4. Transfer the coated flowers and leaves to a rack lined with greaseproof paper and put in a warm place to dry. Store in an airtight container for up to a year, and use to decorate your cakes and puddings.

TOP TIPS

- You can use any edible flowers with this recipe, and there are three ways to tell which ones qualify: (a) you can make wine or cook with the flower, e.g. roses, nasturtiums, pansies;

(b) you can eat the fruit that the flower comes from, e.g. apple blossom; (c) the flower is part of a herb, e.g. chives, rosemary, thyme.

- If you coat mint leaves as described above, you can serve them as unusual and delicious after-dinner mints.

Scones

When it comes to making scones, there can be no greater expert than Richard Hunt, executive chef at the Grand Hotel in Torquay. He was six years old when he baked his first scone, and he has since produced over 150,000 of them for the Grand, sometimes making 8000 a day. His recipe below makes ten scones and produces fantastic results every time.

YOU WILL NEED

- 500 g plain flour
- 70 g caster sugar
- 2 tsp baking powder
- 70 g milk powder
- 60 g butter
- 250 ml buttermilk
- ½ tsp salt
- Beaten egg, to glaze

1. Preheat the oven to 210°C/Gas 7 and line a baking sheet with parchment.
2. Put the flour, sugar, baking powder, milk powder and butter in a large bowl. Rub together with your fingertips so the mixture turns cream-coloured and slightly crumbly. The odd fleck of butter is not a bad thing.
3. Add the buttermilk and salt, stir well, then bring together with your hands to form a firm ball of dough.
4. Knead the dough lightly for 10–15 seconds, no more, otherwise it will be tough, then press it out with your hands to a thickness of 4 cm. (It's important to do this without flouring the dough or the work surface. See also Top Tips.)
5. Using an 8 cm cutter, stamp out circles – a quick downward cut without twisting will give you the best rise in the oven.
6. Place the scones on the prepared baking sheet, a few centimetres apart. Brush the tops with the beaten egg, then bake for 15–20 minutes, until risen and lightly coloured.
7. Serve warm with jam and lashings of clotted cream on top.

TOP TIPS

- When rolling out the scone dough, don't beat it into submission. Use the rolling pin lightly, or gently press out the dough using your hands.

- When baking scones, trust the oven. Don't be constantly opening it and poking around.

- Scones freeze extremely well (for up to six months), provided you put them in an airtight container. To serve, defrost them at room temperature, then put them in the oven at 150°C/Gas 3 for 5–6 minutes, until heated through.

Kirstie's
Damson Jam

Damson Jam

Victoria Cranfield taught me how to make chutney. So when I was entering the Devon County Show competition for cream teas, there was only one person on speed dial to teach me how to make the jam. Damsons are very flavourful and high in pectin, a natural setting agent, so they make a terrific jam. This recipe fills 8–9 jars.

YOU WILL NEED

- 2.7 kg damsons
- 450 ml orange juice
- Zest of 1 orange
- 2.7 kg sugar

1. First sterilise your jam jars. Preheat your oven to its lowest setting, then place the jars upside down in it for 30 minutes. Also, place a saucer in the fridge to chill – you'll need this later to test for setting point.
2. Meanwhile, wash the damsons and remove the stalks. Put the fruit into a large stainless steel saucepan, add the orange juice and zest, and cook over a medium heat until the fruit is soft. Stir occasionally, pushing the damsons against the sides of the pan to release the stones. They will rise to the top and you can then remove them with a slotted spoon.
3. Once you're confident all the stones have been removed, add the sugar to the fruit and bring to the boil, then simmer until all the sugar has dissolved.
4. Now test for setting point: take the pan off the heat and put half a teaspoonful of the jam on your chilled saucer; allow to cool, then push with your finger. If it wrinkles, the jam is ready.
5. Carefully ladle the mixture into the sterilised jars, filling them as near to the top as possible. Place a waxed disc on the surface straight away, then seal and label.

Garden Pickles

If, like me, you grow your own, I'm sure you sometimes find yourself overwhelmed with gluts of fruit or vegetables as summer comes to an end. If you can't face any more cucumber salads or stewed plums for a while, pickling is a great way to save them for later. Pickles are super simple and quick to make, and work for almost any fruit and veg, which means you can enjoy your garden produce all year round.

Here are recipes by Louisa Carter for three of my favourites – pickled summer cucumbers, spiced pickled plums and, for the grown-ups, blackberry vodka. This last one might not sound like a pickle, but it is, with vodka taking the place of the vinegar used in the others. Use it to make knock-your-socks-off martinis, which are perfect for parties all year round.

Pickled Summer Cucumbers

Makes 2–3 large jars

YOU WILL NEED

- 3 large cucumbers, washed and dried
- 2 medium onions
- 2 tbsp salt
- 600 ml white wine vinegar
- 250 g caster sugar
- 1 tsp fennel seeds
- 1 tsp coriander seeds

1. Thinly slice the cucumbers and onions, sprinkle with the salt and arrange in layers in a colander. Cover with a plate and weigh down (with a few tins of beans or somesuch) for 3–4 hours. Pour off the excess liquid.
2. Meanwhile, sterilise your jars (see page 135).
3. Heat the vinegar and sugar in a saucepan until the sugar has dissolved. Add the spices and boil for 10 minutes.
4. Layer the cucumber and onions into your jars and pour over the hot syrup to completely cover the contents. Make sure there are no air bubbles, then cover with a wax disc and fasten the lids tightly. Leave for at least a week in a cool, dark, airy place.

Note: Thinly sliced red or green cabbage or sliced and blanched green beans can be used instead of cucumbers.

Spiced Pickled Plums

Makes about 2 large jars

YOU WILL NEED

- 500 g unblemished plums, washed and dried
- 300 ml red wine vinegar
- 200 g soft brown sugar
- 4 black peppercorns
- 3 cloves
- 1 cinnamon stick

1. First sterilise your jars (see page 135).
2. Meanwhile, prick the plums all over with a clean pin.
3. Heat the vinegar and sugar in a saucepan until the sugar has dissolved, then add the spices and boil for 10 minutes.
4. Pack the plums into your jars and pour in enough hot syrup to completely cover the fruit. Make sure there are no air bubbles, then cover with a wax disc and fasten the lids tightly. Leave for at least a week in a cool, dark, airy place, but a month or two is better.

Note: The plums can be replaced with redcurrants, blackcurrants or cherries. Larger stone fruits, such as apricots, peaches or nectarines, should be blanched, peeled and halved, then poached in the hot syrup for 3 minutes before being packed into jars.

Blackberry Vodka

Makes 2 x 1 litre bottles

YOU WILL NEED

- 600 g unblemished blackberries, washed and drained
- 300 g caster sugar
- 1 vanilla pod, split in half lengthways (optional)
- 1.5–2 litres vodka

1. First sterilise your bottles (see page 135).
2. Fill the bottles two-thirds full with the blackberries, then divide the sugar evenly between them. Add the vanilla pod, if using, then pour in enough vodka to reach 5 mm below the neck of the bottle. Seal and shake gently, then store in a cool, dark, airy place. Shake gently every day until the sugar has dissolved, then gently shake once a month for at least 3 months. The blackberry vodka gets better with time and should keep for several years.
3. When ready, strain the vodka into sterilised bottles if you want to keep it. Otherwise, drink straight away, using the fruit as a boozy tart filling or topping for ice cream.

Note: You can replace the blackberries with blackcurrants, cherries, plums or any soft fruit, and use gin instead of vodka.

Garden Crafts

I've always believed that the garden should be treated just like any other room in the house. It's a completely versatile space that can be used for playing, relaxing, entertaining and eating. There are so many clever ways of bringing it to life and making it a comfortable place, whatever the weather, and of course in my opinion crafts are integral to getting it right. They can bring that extra bit of sparkle and interest, and this chapter shows you how.

My parents always encouraged us to help in the garden when we were growing up because they are so green-fingered and passionate about gardening. Right now, as a busy working mum, I don't have the time or the energy that I'd like to devote to gardening, but I am still enthusiastic to learn. My garden at Meadowgate suffered forty years of neglect, but has come on leaps and bounds since I bought the house. That's the thing about gardening – it doesn't have to take years to produce an attractive and welcoming space; the effects can be almost immediate. You can sow a few seeds and in three months have plants and flowers sprouting galore. So roll your sleeves up and get out there: you'll be really glad you did.

One of the most wonderful things about crafting for the garden is that you can use natural and recycled materials to great effect. Shells, rocks, driftwood and stones can be bought from garden centres and online and arranged into attractive groups to encourage wildlife, or used simply as interesting features among the greenery. Large stones can be painted with the names of plants and used as markers, or get the children to decorate them. They'll love doing this and it will bring a very personal touch to the garden.

I highly recommend getting your children to make the birdseed cakes on page 157. This project is a fun and easy thing to do together that will get them out into the garden, encourage them to take an interest in the birds who come down to feast, and is a great way to help the environment. My children have endless hours of fun trying to identify all the different types of bird that visit our garden.

A patio area is the perfect outside place to indulge your craft habit, particularly if you like to have containers filled with different plants to suit the season. To my mind you can't go far wrong in a garden with a wooden box. It's a simple but lovely way of displaying flowers, shrubs or herbs, and can be decorated in any way you like to complement your colour scheme. Old wooden crates make terrific containers and I love personalising them to my taste. The project on page 145 shows how you can customise your box with a lick of paint and some basic wood-carving tools, and I think the result is really lovely. Go on, try it – it's easier than you think.

Once you've got your containers sorted, your garden needs furniture to make it complete. I love picking up old metal or wooden chairs and tables at car boot sales and junk shops for this purpose. However rickety they are, you can usually transform them with a bit of elbow grease, plus a wire brush, sandpaper and some outdoor paint. They don't have to be all the same either. I love mixing and matching old finds – it gives the garden more personality and interest. Even if you're normally conservative with colour indoors, be bold outside. It's a great place to experiment with the brighter shades on the colour chart, and you'll be amazed at how effective they look against a green backdrop.

Another way of transforming old furniture for the garden is with mosaic, and I've been hooked on this intricate, detailed craft ever since I was introduced to it a few years ago. The art of mosaic has been practised for thousands of years, first by the Greeks, who passed their skills to the Romans, and they in turn brought it to Britain in the first century AD. I adore the fact that you can use just about any material to make the design of your choice. Broken crockery, bits of glass, pebbles, jewellery, buttons and shells are all suitable, and you can also buy ready-made ceramic tiles and squares. Whilst you might be sad that you've broken your favourite serving bowl, think of it as an opportunity

to make a mosaic and enjoy it in a different form for many years to come. For a great starter project, try your hand at the mosaic chair on page 153.

Want yet more decorative ideas for your garden? Think about introducing objects made of willow. It's a fantastic natural material available in a range of colours and can be used for everything from baskets to garden furniture. Willow working is one of the most ancient crafts – the British Museum holds a complete wicker basket dating from 3000 BC – and is believed to be contemporary with the first chipping of flint into arrowheads. Sadly, the willow industry has been in decline for many years, largely because willow weaving is so labour intensive and therefore expensive. It's no surprise that cheap cardboard, plastic and other modern materials have taken over, but it's a great pity because willow is a beautiful material, extremely durable and can be repaired. Investing in it and using it to craft is therefore well worth the time and effort.

Different types of willow can be foraged all over the countryside, or can be bought from specialist growers. Apart from that, all you really need is a pair of secateurs. The beautiful nesting box on page 165 is a great project to start with.

The final and probably my favourite project in this chapter is one for all the family – making a scarecrow. The humble scarecrow is a familiar site in the British countryside, but in the Middle Ages farmers employed small children to work as crow scarers. The children would run around the fields, clapping blocks of wood to frighten the birds away. Can you imagine anyone getting away with that nowadays? As bubonic plague decimated the population, farmers found there was a shortage of children, so instead they stuffed old clothes on a frame and put the figure up in their field. It did the same job as the children (and cost them less), so the scarecrow became a familiar feature in our countryside.

There you have it: lots of ideas to decorate your garden in ways that capitalise on some great British crafts. You'll have a fantastic time making them, and afterwards you can enjoy a space that is uniquely your own.

 Carved Window Box

All sorts of things make great planters for the garden and I am a huge fan of picking up old wooden boxes and containers at my local reclamation yard and turning them into containers for plants and flowers. For me, it makes the garden much more personal than using the standard plastic containers you can buy everywhere. Also, putting the finishing touches to them makes them uniquely your own.

This project, designed by Jill Alblas, is a perfect example of how, with a bit of effort and a few simple tools, you can transform a plain wooden box into a thing of beauty. Search your shed, local reclamation yard or garden centre for something suitable, then try your hand at carving it. You'll be glad you did.

YOU WILL NEED

- Sandpaper
- Rectangular wooden box
- Paintbrush
- White emulsion paint
- Pencil and ruler
- Tracing paper (optional)
- Rotary tool (Dremel 7700 or 300), with multi chuck and
- carving tip 108
- Acrylic paints (I used cream, raspberry, blue and white)
- Wood glue

1. Start by sanding down your wooden box to give it a smooth finish.
2. Apply matt emulsion so you have a good surface to work on. Leave to dry.
3. Copy the heart, bird and border template below onto the front and ends of the box. You could do this freehand, or expand the images to the size you want on a photocopier, then trace around them and transfer them to your box.

4. Paint the borders cream, the hearts raspberry and the birds blue, making sure you don't paint over the outlines as you'll need these later. Allow to dry.
5. Mix some white paint with blue to make a pastel shade, then paint the background and back of the window box. Leave to dry.
6. Use a pencil and ruler to draw a line along the middle of the borders. Measure and pencil the border at 8 mm intervals to create a check effect.

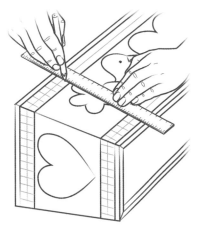

7. Place the multi chuck and carving tip in the rotary tool. Starting with the hearts and birds carve around the outlines. You don't need to apply much pressure: just place the tip in position and gently work around the lines. Next, carve the check effect at the top and bottom of the box. Your pretty, Scandinavian-style window box is now ready to fill with the plants of your choice.

TOP TIPS

- Can't find a ready-made container of the right size? Just make your own. All you need are a few pieces of wood (15 x 2 cm is ideal), a ruler, pencil and sharp handsaw, a mitre to help cut the corners at a 45-degree angle, and some screws to hold it together

- Remember the carpenter's old rule: measure it twice, cut it once.

- Always follow the grain when sanding wood, and use a sanding block (a small piece of wood with the sandpaper wrapped around it) to ensure you sand to the same depth all over.

- If the window box is to be used outside, ensure your paints are weatherproof, and give extra protection by adding a few coats of varnish.

Elderflower Cordial

Having an afternoon to yourself with a crafting project is a real luxury, and what makes it even better is sipping a cool and refreshing drink of elderflower cordial. It's really simple to make, keeps well in a sealed bottle, and in late spring/early summer every hedgerow has the potential to provide you with the essential ingredient. Make it using the following method taught to me by Rosie Davies.

- 6–8 young elderflower heads
- 3–4 large unwaxed lemons
- 1 kg granulated sugar
- 25 g citric acid
- 15 g tartaric acid
- 15 g Epsom salts
- 900 ml boiling water

1. Gently rinse the elderflowers in cold water.
2. Wash and dry the lemons, then grate the rind finely into a very large bowl. Squeeze in the lemon juice, then add the sugar, acids, Epsom salts and elderflowers.
3. Pour on the boiling water and stir until the sugar has completely dissolved. Cover and leave until cold, preferably overnight.
4. Strain through a very fine sieve or muslin, then pour into sterilised bottles (see page 133). Seal tightly and store in a cool place.
5. To serve, dilute the cordial to taste with fizzy water, and serve over ice with a slice or two of lemon, or a sprig of mint floating on top. For grown-ups you could add a shot of gin or vodka, or add it to white wine and sparkling water to make an elderflower spritzer. Once the bottle is open, keep in the fridge.

☙ Mosaic Chair ❧

Mosaic-making is an old and versatile skill that has survived for centuries. I was given my first lesson in it a couple of years ago, and whilst I was initially sceptical about how much I would enjoy it, it turned out to be one of the most exciting crafts that I have ever done. Since then I've had a few more goes, and every time I've been amazed at what can be achieved. I now completely and utterly love mosaics for their detail, and fully appreciate the skill that's involved in making them.

Making a mosaic certainly isn't a quick craft – it takes plenty of time, effort and commitment – but it doesn't take long to get the hang of the basics. Once that's done, you can use mosaics to decorate just about any surface, putting the pieces straight onto an item, or making your design on MDF and attaching it to whatever you fancy. Here is a project for a chair, designed by Jill Alblas, to make a small corner of your garden that bit more special.

YOU WILL NEED

- Chair with a circular flat seat
- Pencil and ruler
- Pair of compasses
- About 250 mosaic tiles, 1 cm square, in brown,
- pale pink and yellow
- About 250 mosaic tiles, 5 mm square, in deep pink, beige, turquoise and brown
- Mosaic glue
- Mosaic grout
- Mosaic cutters or small wire cutters
- Sponge
- Soft cloth
- Craft tweezers

Remember before you start to protect your clothes with an apron or old shirt.

1. Refer to illustration 1. Mark the centre of the seat. Use a pencil and ruler to divide the seat into four equal sections, then repeat to make eight equal sections. Place the point of your compasses in the centre and draw two circles, one inside the other: the smaller one has radius of 3 cm, and the larger one a 7 cm radius. These pencilled circles and segments will enable you to mosaic the seat symmetrically.
2. Following the manufacturers' instructions, apply some mosaic glue around the perimeter of the larger circle and stick 5 mm deep pink tiles to it. Leave a gap of about 1 mm between each tile.
3. Apply glue around the perimeter of the smaller circle and stick 5 mm beige tiles to it.
4. Refer to illustration 4. Mosaic the centre of the seat by gluing four concentric rows of 5 mm deep pink tiles inside the beige-tiled circle. Fill in the middle with a few extra tiles.
5. Still referring to illustration 4, glue 1 cm pale pink tiles around the deep pink tiles surrounding the larger circle. Follow this with a row of 1 cm brown tiles, then another row of pale pink tiles.

6. Glue 1 cm brown tiles around the outside edge of the seat. Follow these with a row of 1 cm pale pink tiles, then another row of brown.

7. Refer to illustration 7. Arrange 5 mm turquoise tiles in a petal shape – the inner dotted lines indicate the centre of the petal and will help you to arrange the tiles evenly. Glue the tiles in place. Repeat to make eight mosaic petals.

8. Using your cutters, snip some 1 cm yellow tiles into a variety of sizes and shapes. Glue these pieces between the petals.

9. Refer to illustration 9 for the cross pattern. Following an outer dotted line, glue 2 small beige tiles, 1 turquoise, 1 deep pink, 1 turquoise and 2 beige tiles in a line. Glue 1 small turquoise tile either side of the deep pink tile. Repeat this pattern on the remaining dotted lines. If you like, you can glue another one or two of these arrangements in between.

10. Snip some more yellow tiles into various shapes and sizes and use to fill between the tiles to complete your mosaic. Leave to dry in a warm room for 24 hours.

11. Grout the chair according to the manufacturers' instructions, then gently rub a damp sponge over the whole mosaic. Leave to dry, then polish with a soft cloth.

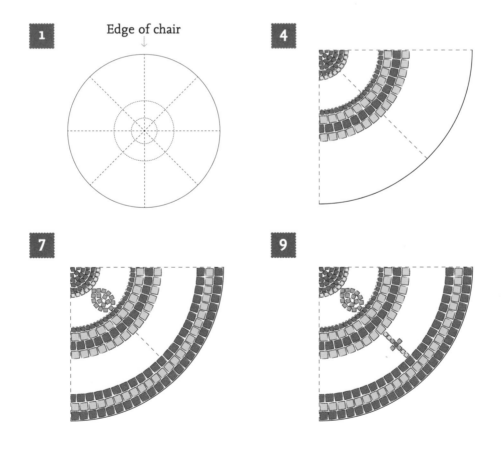

- Take your time when marking up the seat in pencil. Doing this accurately will save you a lot of time later and ensure your finished mosaic looks great.

- Craft tweezers are invaluable for picking up and positioning the tiles, so if you are serious about mosaic-making, they are definitely worth investing in.

Birdseed Cakes

When I'm down in Devon at Meadowgate, there is nothing nicer than looking out of the kitchen window and seeing birds merrily hopping around in the garden looking for food. These birdseed cakes are quite literally child's play, and the kids will take great pleasure in helping you make them, and then watching for hours as the birds come down to feast.

Although the recipe suggests making them with wild birdseed mix, you can use a wide range of different foods, such as unsalted peanuts, dried fruit, oatmeal, grated cheese, cake crumbs or a mixture of all these things. Just remember that the rule is one-third fat to two-thirds mixture.

I shape the cakes by hand, but they can also be made in plastic containers, such as empty yoghurt pots. Don't use your best freezer boxes because the containers usually have to be broken to get the cakes out. The quantities below make 3–4 cakes.

YOU WILL NEED

- Empty plastic containers, such as yoghurt pots or vending machine cups
- Wooden skewers
- Scissors
- Garden string
- 1 cup lard, at room temperature
- 2 cups wild birdseed mix

1. Take a plastic container and use a skewer to make a hole in the bottom. Cut a piece of string about three times longer than the container and fold it in half. Push the loop through the hole so it's sticking outside the container (the point of a wooden skewer will help you). The loop must be long enough to hang the finished cake from a tree.
2. Place a skewer across the top of the container and tie the open ends of the string around it.
3. Put the lard in a pan and heat gently until fully melted. Stir in the birdseed mixture. It should look greasy but have no puddles of liquid fat. Take off the heat and allow to cool and firm up slightly (you don't want it to melt the plastic containers).
4. Fill the containers with the mixture, pushing it down firmly, then leave to set in the fridge.
5. When the mixture has set, carefully remove it from the container (you might have to break the pot). Trim the ends of the skewer, which will act as a perch for the birds. Your birdseed cake is now ready to hang in the garden.

TOP TIPS

- Try to avoid putting the cakes out on really hot days because they will melt. If you must do this, perhaps because you're going away, hang them over the lawn and the birds can get the melted food from there.
- Different seeds attract different birds, so do some research and make your cakes accordingly.

Scarecrow

It's a lovely sight when you're driving through the countryside to see a scarecrow standing in a field doing its job. Making them is even more fun, as I found out when I visited Redhills Community Primary School. They helped me with my entry for the scarecrow competition at the Chagford Show, and they did the most fantastic job. I couldn't have done it without them – and here I am sharing their method.

YOU WILL NEED

- Handsaw
- 2 chunky pieces of wood for the base, plus 4 narrower supports
- 2 thinnish pieces of wood for the 'body', the taller one about 30 cm shorter than you want the scarecrow to be; the other one about half the length
- Screws and screwdriver
- Mitre, to cut 45-degree angles
- Old pair of tights
- Straw or newspaper
- Scraps of old fabric
- Twine
- Old clothes (trousers, waistcoat, shirt, handkerchief, gloves, hat and wellies)
- Hessian sack
- Scissors
- Staple gun
- Safety pins
- Needle and thread
- Old pillowcase
- Assorted buttons
- Thick wool, red and green
- Cardboard (optional)
- Wig (optional)

1. First make the base. Cut a square notch in the middle of one piece of wood and a matching notch in the other so that they slot together.
2. Now make the frame for the body. Cut a square notch in the tall piece of wood about 30 cm below where the head will go. Cut a matching notch in the middle of a cross-beam that will form the shoulders (or shoulders and outstretched arms). Screw together.
3. Insert a long screw through the bottom of the base and into the body upright.
4. Cut four smaller pieces of wood with a 45-degree angle at each end and screw to the base and upright as supports.

5. Stuff a pair of tights with straw, newspaper or fabric, then tie at the top with twine.
6. Put the filled tights inside a pair of old trousers, which have been frayed and had holes cut in the knees.
7. Take a large hessian sack, cut a hole in the centre of the stitched end and hang it over the frame. Use a staple gun to attach it to the wood.
8. Using safety pins, attach the filled trousers to the bottom of the hessian sack.
9. Stuff straw in the holes of the trousers so that the straw sticks out.
10. Fill the sack with straw, newspaper or old fabric to fill out the 'body'.
11. Stitch large patches of fabric scraps onto the waistcoat.
12. Put an old shirt, then the waistcoat over the filled-out body and frame.
13. To make the face, half-fill the pillowcase with straw and tie some twine around it.
14. Now make eyes by placing small buttons on top of larger buttons and sewing them onto the pillowcase. Stitch scraps of fabric above the buttons for eyebrows. Sew a line with thick red wool to create a mouth.
15. Cut a triangle of orange fabric to make a carrot nose. Fold it in half, stitch along the length, then stuff with straw and stitch the end closed. Attach some green wool to the flat end like carrot leaves. Stitch the finished nose to the pillowcase.
16. Slightly loosen the twine around the pillowcase, put the head on top of the frame and tie tightly around the frame to hold it in place. Attach the bottom of the pillowcase to the hessian body with safety pins.
17. Tie a handkerchief around the neck.
18. Roll up the cardboard, tie with twine and insert into the sleeves of the shirt. Alternatively, stuff the sleeves with newspaper, straw or old fabric.
19. Fill a pair of gloves with stuffing and attach to the ends of the sleeves with safety pins.
20. Place the bottom of the trousers inside the wellingtons and stuff the tops with straw.
21. Add a wig or straw for hair, then sit a hat on top and attach with safety pins.

TOP TIPS

- Safety pins will hold your scarecrow together, but if you want to make it last longer, use stitches with the pins too.

- You can weatherproof your scarecrow by putting your straw or newspaper stuffing inside a bin bag.

- If you don't want to do the woodwork elements of this project, you could sit your scarecrow on an old chair.

Willow Nesting Box

Willow weaving is a wonderful craft – natural, environmentally friendly and long-lasting. I find the smell and texture of willow addictive, and another person who is passionate about it is Annemarie O'Sullivan. Formerly a primary school teacher, she enrolled on a one-day basket-making course and has never looked back. What Annemarie makes is contemporary and fresh. She's bringing willow back into the modern age. Try this nesting box to whet your willow appetite.

NOTES

- The thick end of the willow rod is called the 'butt', the thin end is called the 'tip'. Always join butt to butt and tip to tip.
- Make sure you buy British willow (it's always quoted in imperial sizes). Starter packs can be ordered online. Check out the Basketmakers Association (www.basketassoc.org) to find a supplier near you.
- Willow with its bark on will need to be soaked for one day per foot (5 ft lengths for five days; 3 ft lengths for three days). Buff willow, which has had its bark removed, will need to be soaked for only an hour in hot water.

YOU WILL NEED

- 5 ft rods flexible willow, for stakes
- 3 ft rods flexible willow, for weaving
- Pair of compasses and a pencil
- Ruler or tape measure
- Lid from old cardboard shoebox, folds opened out
- Skewer
- String
- Weight, such as a brick, to keep the structure in place while weaving
- Secateurs
- Flat stone, as a base inside the basket for the bird to build a nest on

1. Soak your willow as necessary (see notes on previous page).
2. Using the compasses and pencil, draw a circle with a radius of 7.25 cm on your cardboard – you need a diameter of 14.5 cm. (You could draw around a plate if you have one of the right size.)
3. Make marks 3 cm apart around your circle to show where the stakes will go. You should end up with 15 marks. (It is always essential to have an odd number so that the weaving pattern will work out.) Push a skewer through each mark to make a hole.
4. Take the butt end of each stake and push it about 20 cm through a hole in the cardboard. When the stakes are all in place, use some string to tie the bunch together at the tips. This will help to keep them steady while you complete the base.
5. Secure the stakes on the underside of the cardboard by kinking each one about 18 cm from the butt end. Then bend one piece down past four stakes to the right. Keeping this rod in place, move to the right and bend the next stake down past four stakes to the right. Continue in this way around the circle.

6. Push the cardboard against the lattice-work base and set it on a table with the weight inside. Begin the weaving with a tip.
7. To join in a new rod, use secateurs to cut the finishing butt end so that it sits neatly behind a stake. Place the butt end of a new weaving rod in the next space, touching the old butt end. Join in a new rod by overlapping the new tip on top of the old tip. Remember, the rule for joining is tip to tip and butt to butt.
8. You can undo the string at the top when the stakes feel as though they are secure. To stop the stakes from caving inwards, pull them gently upright as you weave around them.
9. When the weaving is about 10 cm tall, the doorway of the feeder needs to be made. Take a thin weaving rod, turn it back on itself and weave in the opposite direction. When the rod returns to two stakes before the original turn, the weaving should turn around again, leaving a space between the two turns.

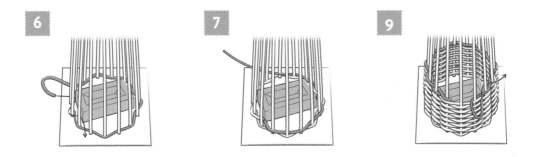

10. When the space is about 5 cm tall, resume the usual way of weaving in complete circles. Continue until the weaving becomes too tight. Finish the weaving with a tip.

11. Now make the binding. Place a scrap piece of willow in the bunch of stakes, hold it tight and add the butt end of a thin and flexible weaving rod to the bunch. Wind the weaver tightly around the bunch 4–5 times, making sure it goes below the previous round each time so that the binding sits neatly. Remove the scrap piece of willow, slide the tip end of the binder through the space where it was and pull through tightly.

12. Cut the tops off the stakes and trim any loose ends. Cut the stake in the doorway about 1 cm beyond the weaving.

13. Undo the base by gently pulling out some of the folded ends. The base will unravel and the cardboard can be removed. Put your flat stone inside the basket. With the basket upside down and using a tip end, begin weaving to fill the space around the base. Add as many weaving rods as you need until the space left by the cardboard has been filled.

14. Complete the base in the same way you did in step 5.

Flower Crafts

I've said it before and I'll say it again: I love flowers. Having them in the house brightens up even the dreariest of days and, depending on the time of year, looking out of the window to see a patch of daffodils or a cluster of pansies always puts a smile on my face. I adore having flowers around the house in as many rooms as possible because their different colours and scents bring an unbeatable individuality. They go a long way to making a house a home, and are essential if you're trying to sell your house. They show your potential buyers that your particular pile of bricks and mortar is a well-loved home and one that they could enjoy too. (You see – I'm never off property duty.)

In these cost-conscious days, it must be admitted that buying flowers is a luxury, so when I was overhauling the neglected garden at Meadowgate, I was really keen to plant flowers suitable for cutting and arranging around the house (without leaving the garden bereft, of course). If you have a garden, do try growing your own. Forget-me-nots, aquilegias and poppies, for example, grow like weeds and self-seed, so they come back every year. Sweet peas are also fantastically easy to grow and produce heavenly scented flowers right through the summer. If you don't have space for flower beds in your garden, why not make a pretty border of, say, marigolds, campanula and alyssum, around your other plants or vegetables? All you need is a few packets of seeds, a bag of potting compost and some seedling trays and you're away. You'll be amazed at how much money you can save and how much pleasure arranging your very own blooms will give you. Think of your green credentials too: they haven't had to travel far to make it to your kitchen table.

If you're nervous about planting, I recommend taking advice from the experts. You need to plant your garden so that you have different flowers popping up at different times of the year. Plan out what you are putting in before you buy up the garden centre. That way you will be guaranteed to have flowers all year round. For a greater chance of success, stick with what is native to the local area and the UK, and let's keep our home-grown flowers flourishing.

If you simply don't have the time or energy to devote to gardening, use your imagination and look around the garden for other colourful growth you can bring indoors. A bit of foliage and some berries or rosehips can look pretty stunning in a bowl. Failing that, or if you don't have a garden at all, go for a walk in the countryside and see what you can pick from the hedgerows. Remember, there are some rules when picking wild: never trespass and don't take flowers from a nature reserve or a protected site without permission. It's best to check out who owns the land before you start picking because some species are protected. And finally, leave some flowers for others to enjoy too.

While you're on your foraging expedition, keep your eyes open for elder bushes. In late spring and early summer they produce frothy flowerheads that not only look pretty, but can also be used to make a wonderfully fragrant cordial (see page 149).

Now we've got our flower sources sorted, let's talk arranging. Flower arrangements have always played an important part in festivals, religious ceremonies and celebrations of all kinds. Early Egyptian paintings and sculptures found in ancient tombs depict flowers in vases, and every culture seems to have its own symbolism and conventions surrounding flowers. Even today, certain flowers have particular connotations – roses for anniversaries, lilies for funerals – but these old ideas have pretty much fallen by the wayside and nowadays you can use any flowers you want on any occasion.

Flower arranging is a real art and can be a bit scary to the novice, but believe me, anyone can do it and it doesn't have to be complicated to look great. It first became

really popular in Britain after the publication of Gertrude Jekyll's 'Flower Decoration in the House' in 1907. Jekyll, a noted garden designer who often collaborated with the architect Edwin Lutyens, put forward the idea that flower decorations could be planned and designed to improve the quality of a room, and I couldn't agree more.

To my mind, flower arranging is a particularly satisfying craft because the results are pretty instantaneous. However, I do advise you not to get bogged down in the technical terms of floral design. When people start talking line, form or proportion it all sounds a bit scary and difficult. On the other hand, there is absolutely no harm in speaking to experts or learning a few of the rules if you can – they can all go some way to improving your technique. The main thing is not to let anyone tell you that putting some flowers in a vase and making them look pretty isn't 'proper' flower arranging. It's actually a great way to start learning how to handle flowers and put them in place. You might not be ready to win prizes at the local country show, but if your arrangement looks pretty to you, that's absolutely fine.

If you feel you are not ready to go freestyle and do your own arrangements, the projects in this chapter will help to inspire you and teach you a few tricks. Everything you'll need in the way of equipment – florist's foam, wire and suchlike – can be bought from florists, or is readily available online. In all likelihood, you've probably already got everything you need to get started. For a simple arrangement, all you need is a container – one of my favourites is an old jam jar – and a few flowers and bits of greenery. Remember, almost any type of container can hold flowers. I'm always picking up old jugs and pots at auctions, and I can't pass by an antique shop without popping in to see if there are any gems just waiting to be found. It's the most addictive type of shopping, and you can use your finds to inspire your choice of flowers and the type of arrangement. Likewise, when you know what flowers you want to use, think about the container and where it's going to sit – you don't want a massive vase in the middle of the dining table obscuring your guests. If you're really stuck for containers, ice-cream tubs covered in moss, or tin cans decorated with wrapping paper and a bit of ribbon make beautifully effective vases.

When entertaining, I believe that flowers really finish off a table, but I don't necessarily go for huge formal arrangements. Try the quick and easy table centre on page 179 and your guests will be terribly impressed. If pushed for time, dotting several little vases of flowers around the table can also be very effective. And to make a special occasion that bit more memorable, coordinate the flowers with your party theme or colour scheme and it will look like you've really gone that extra mile.

As I keep advocating, don't be afraid to bend or break a few rules. The garden wreath on page 181, for example, shows that herbs and evergreens combined with seasonal flowers are effective decorations all year round, not just in winter. These circlets date back to ancient Greece and Rome, where they were originally worn as headbands to identify members of different societies, or given as prizes at the early Olympic Games. How they ended up on our front doors is a bit of a mystery, but I'm happy to see the rule subverted about where and when they should be used.

The ancient Greeks also believed that the fragrance of flowers and herbs warded off evil spirits, so they either carried them or attached them to their clothing during weddings, thus starting a tradition that has come down to us in the form of corsages and buttonholes. I think it's a lovely idea to wear a corsage that complements your outfit, and there is a particularly beautiful example for you to try on page 183.

Finally, there's a project that uses a wide variety of dried seedheads to decorate a mirror for use as a table centre (see page 189). With a few candles in the middle, the effect is simple and stunning.

TIPS OF THE TRADE

In my journey through flower arranging I've met some wonderfully creative people and learnt so much from them. One of them was the fantastic floral designer Paul Hawkins, who gave me some tips that I think have definitely helped improve the arrangements I make at home. Bear them in mind and I'm sure they will help you too:

• Always use odd numbers of flowers in your arrangements, usually three or five stems.

• Flowers grow in groups, so always group them in arrangements rather than spreading them; this gives a spectacular, professional look.

• Always put your foliage into the arrangement first to help you get the basic shape right. The flowers can slot in afterwards.

• Think about your colour scheme before buying any flowers to make sure the two go together.

• Ideally, make your arrangement in situ so you can see exactly how it will work in the room.

• Buy as many flowers as you can afford. Even if that's not very many, it's what you do with them that counts.

• Don't be a flower snob: some well-arranged carnations can look just as good as more expensive flowers.

Petite Floral Exhibit

Part of the challenge in the flower-arranging competition at the Cornwall County Show was to come up with a 'petite exhibit' – a flower arrangement that does not exceed 25 cm in width, depth and height. To help me prepare, I met floral designer Sioned Rowlands, who taught me a traditional triangular-shaped design. It can be made in a small jar or a teacup, so would look lovely on a kitchen windowsill, in a small bathroom or a guest bedroom.

YOU WILL NEED

- Knife or scissors
- Florist's foam (Oasis)
- Small container, such as a glass jar
- Pot tape (waterproof plastic, for securing florist's foam in containers)
- Foliage, such as ivy and hebe
- Flowers, such as spray roses, marguerites, lavender and heather
- Filler, such as alchemilla

1. Cut the florist's foam to fit inside your container.
2. Put the foam to soak (see technique, page 181), then place in the container and secure with pot tape. Always take the tape around the container and then back on itself to make sure it sticks.
3. Start arranging the foliage to create the outer shape of your design and cover the edge of the container. All material should be placed as if coming from one point in the centre of the foam.
4. Place your main flowers in a line, graduating from a bud at the top to an open rose in the centre, then buds tapering to the side. To add interest, place another flower, such as marguerites, through the design to the other side, again with similar distances between them, this time pushing the stems a little deeper so that the flower heads are lower than the roses to give depth to your arrangement.
5. Filler material, such as alchemilla, should be placed in between the flower heads, keeping within the overall shape and softening all edges to keep the arrangement loose and give a lovely natural country feel.

TOP TIPS

- Soak foliage and flowers for at least 12 hours before inserting them into the foam.
- Try to be precise when putting flowers into the foam because if you have to take them out again, the foam will start disintegrating and won't hold them securely.
- Use flowers with a firm stem so that they are easier to insert in the foam.

❧ Table Centre ❧

Arranging flowers for a table centre, rather than just sticking them in a vase and plonking them in the middle of the table, can be slightly daunting, but it's worth the extra effort. It looks good, will impress guests and add that special finishing touch to any dinner party. And a properly thought-through arrangement, like the beautiful design opposite by floral decorator Paul Hawkins, needn't cost the earth either. I recommend you to make friends with your florist and find out what's in season, or take a look in the garden and use what's right on your doorstep.

YOU WILL NEED

- Knife or scissors
- Round block of florist's foam (Oasis)
- Round bowl
- Seasonal flowers (our arrangement includes roses, hydrangeas, lilies, peonies and eryngium, also known as sea holly)

1. Cut the foam to the diameter of your bowl but do not reduce the thickness. Place in water and leave until it is fully saturated (see technique, page 181).
2. Take your bowl and wedge in the foam – it should be about 5 cm taller than the bowl.
3. Remove any foliage and thorns from the roses, then trim the stems to a length slightly shorter than the depth of the foam, cutting the ends at an angle. Prepare the rest of the flowers in a similar way, but simply trim the stems of the foliage.
4. Insert three roses, evenly spaced, into the foam. Fill the rest of the space with the remaining flowers and foliage until the foam is completely covered.

TOP TIPS

- Sprigs of herbs can be interspersed with your foliage to create a lovely fragrance.

- Always use odd numbers of flowers as (paradoxically) it makes for a more balanced arrangement.

- Our arrangement has no foliage, but feel free to add whatever takes your fancy. Holly, ivy and rosehips look wonderful in winter arrangements. At other times of year, use whatever greenery you can find in your garden or country lanes.

- Top up the water in the foam daily to make sure your flowers last longer. To make this easier, cut a V-shaped notch in the foam before inserting it into the container. Water can then be poured into the notch without it spilling over.

Garden Wreath

I always get really excited at Christmas time when I hang my wreath on the front door; it feels like putting a cherry on top of a well-iced cake. But why wait for Christmas? This beautifully simple wreath, designed by Paul Hawkins, is made with a selection of early summer flowers and greenery, and can be hung indoors or out to lift your spirits every time you see it. The wreath is easy to make and costs a fraction of a shop-bought one. Pick your herbs and flowers depending on the season, combining both dried and fresh in whatever way you want.

YOU WILL NEED

- Florist's foam ring with plastic back
- Cable tie, for hanging up (optional)
- Florist's wire
- Wire cutters
- Floristry scissors (optional)
- 4 types of herbs or flowers, stems about 10 cm long (we've used fresh bay, green hydrangea heads, eucalyptus and lavender)

1. Fill your sink with water, place the foam ring face down on the surface and leave for about 5 minutes. It's important to let the foam draw in the water naturally because if you force it under the water or run water over it, the water will be soaked up unevenly. and leave dry spots. You'll know you've soaked the foam adequately once it submerges almost completely with only around 5 mm showing above the water.
2. Loop a cable tie or some florist's wire around the foam for hanging it later.
3. Mark your foam into quarters by scoring lightly with the blunt side of your scissors. Each quarter is reserved for one type of flower or herb.
4. Strip off any excess leaves at the bottom of the stems, then cut the stems at an angle; this makes them easier to insert into the foam and allows them to soak up the water more efficiently.
5. Group the herbs/flowers into bunches of three or five stems. Take a piece of florist's wire about 15 cm long and bend one end into a 'U' shape. Put a bunch of herbs/flowers inside the 'U', then twist the wire around to secure, leaving a 'tail' of it hanging down.
6. Always plan your arrangement before you start inserting the bunches because you can't reuse a hole once it's made. The cells will be crushed and won't be able to provide water to a new stem; also, unused holes act as air pockets, making the foam less effective.
7. Working a quarter at a time with each herb/flower individually, insert the stems firmly into the foam without wiggling them, making sure you fan them all in the same direction, like a Catherine wheel. The cut ends must be in constant contact with the foam to ensure they can soak up enough water, so don't poke them all the way through the foam.
8. When the ring is covered with herbs/flowers, hang it over a bowl or outside until the water stops dripping, then hang in the desired place.

✣ Corsage ✣

Why should the fragrance and beauty of flowers be confined to the house or garden? If you are going somewhere special, such as a wedding, I firmly believe there's nothing nicer than finishing off your outfit with some flowers. Call me a traditionalist, but in my view it's absolutely lovely when you complete your look with a matching corsage.

As floral decorator Paul Hawkins shows below, corsages are incredibly easy to make yourself, though I suggest you practise yours before the big day. They're also lovely as presents, so you could offer to make them for the bridal party as your wedding gift to the bride and groom.

The corsage shown here can include up to three roses and five ivy leaves for a woman. For a man it's called a buttonhole, but is basically the same on a smaller, simpler scale. You can use one rose (or other flower) as the centrepiece, plus one ivy leaf or, say, one sprig of rosemary.

Remember that this project can be adapted to use your favourite flower.

YOU WILL NEED

• Scissors
• 1 white rose
• Florist's wire
• Wire cutters
• Ivy or herb sprig
• Florist's paper gutter tape
• Pearl or diamanté pin

1. Cut the stem of the rose to leave a 7.5 cm stalk.
2. Cut a piece of florist's wire to the full length of your rose, then push the wire up the stem and right into the flower head.
3. Place the ivy behind the rose so that it frames the flower.
4. Take the rose between your thumb and index finger. Beginning at the top, wrap the paper gutter tape around the stem, turning it as you go so that the tape goes on evenly. (The heat of your hand makes the tape stick to the stem.) When you reach the bottom of the stem, go all the way back up, wrapping the tape around again. Make sure the whole stem is covered.
5. Use a beautiful pin to attach the corsage to your clothing.

Floral Line Design

As someone who's only ever done my own flower arrangements at home, entering a competition was terrifying enough, but deciding to put myself up against experts was even worse. Yes, that's what I was doing at the Cornwall Show. To add to the terror, the competition involved being given a box of flowers and only two hours to produce a potentially award-winning arrangement. I really am a glutton for punishment!

To make sure I was fully prepared for this test, I needed help, and, luckily for me, Tan Strong, queen of competitive flower arranging, came to my rescue. Tan took me through her 'line design', which is very basic yet produces lovely results. The idea is to have a clear line of flowers in the centre, with groupings of other elements, such as fruit and berries, around the base. I was amazed at the results and really recommend you try it.

YOU WILL NEED

- Knife
- 1 block florist's foam
- Shallow container, e.g. casserole dish, salad bowl, ceramic vase – whatever you can find
- Scissors
- 4 small sprigs hebe or similar bushy foliage
- 3–4 heuchera leaves, or other interesting leaves from the garden
- 3–4 large ivy leaves
- 2 limes
- Wooden kebab sticks
- 2 red plums and/or cherries
- 5–6 roses, various head sizes
- Few cymbidium orchid flowers
- Small amounts of moss
- German pins or small pieces of bent wire
- 4 stems green hypericum berries
- Decorative wire

1. Cut the florist's foam to fit your container with a knife, then place the foam in a large bowl of water. Allow it to become wet and sink naturally, without pressing it under the surface: this prevents any 'air locks'. When it is saturated and has changed colour, place it in the container without pressing to make it fit.
2. Re-cut the stems of each item of foliage, then make groupings of them around the container.

3. Cut the limes in half, pierce with a wooden kebab stick, then place a cluster of them in the foam.

4. Place sticks in the plums and position next to a green grouping of leaves so they will be seen clearly.

5. Remove the lower foliage from the roses and arrange the flowers on the table in order of size, from smallest bud to largest bloom.

6. Take the smallest rosebud or bloom and place it in the centre of your foam. Its height should be approximately one and a half times the width of your container.

7. Follow this with a slightly larger flower, but cut the stem shorter. Repeat this until you have a straight, central line of colour, with the largest bloom at the base. Do not be afraid of cutting your shortest stem quite short, as this tends to extend the life of the flower.

8. Add further flowers, such as orchids, between the foliage groups to create interest from all sides.

9. Turn your arrangement around to ensure that none of the foam is visible. If it is, conceal with a small piece of moss secured with a German pin or a piece of bent wire

10. Remove the berries from the hypericum and thread onto a length of decorative wire. Add to the arrangement by fixing each end into the foam.

TOP TIPS

• Adapt this design to combine whatever you have from the garden with a few bought flowers. Check what's in season to ensure economical choices. Here are a few seasonal ideas:

Spring – irises and tulips with empty eggshells.

Summer – peonies and roses with cherries and fruits.

Autumn – orange lilies and sunflowers or gerberas with apples and bunches of blackberries.

Winter – bare twigs with a few white roses, fir cones and conifer sprigs.

Christmas – roses, holly, ivy and baubles arranged around a central candle.

• To keep the design looking fresher for longer, spray with water regularly and try to keep the container topped up with water at all times.

Seedhead Mirror

As you might remember, dried-flower arrangements were hugely popular in the 1980s, but have since fallen out of fashion. Paul Hawkins is out to change all that with this beautiful modern arrangement, which doubles as a mirror for the wall and as a table centre. He uses a mixture of dried seedheads, fruits and nuts, which you can either buy or forage.

YOU WILL NEED

- Glue gun
- Mirror, of any shape or size
- Selection of dried seed-heads, nuts and seeds (we used pine cones, lotus heads, poppy heads and hazelnuts, but use whatever you can find or buy at your local craft shop/floristry supplier)
- Tissue paper (optional)
- Spray varnish (optional)
- 1 self-adhesive hanging disc, for wall mounting
- Tea lights or pillar candle, for table centre

1. Begin by heating up your glue gun so it's ready to use.
2. Meanwhile, put your mirror on a work surface. Starting with the larger ingredients, in this case the pine cones, place them in groups of three at various points around the frame (see opposite). Once you have arranged them, glue them to the mirror.
3. Now take the smaller seedheads and, type by type, arrange in groups of three around the frame. When you are happy with the arrangement, glue them in position. Repeat until you have glued all your ingredients to the mirror and the frame is completely covered.
4. To add an extra bit of gloss to the finish, cover the centre of the mirror with tissue paper to protect it, then spray the dried seedheads with varnish. Leave to dry, then remove the tissue.
5. To hang the mirror on the wall, stick the self-adhesive hanging disc on the back according to the manufacturer's instructions.
6. If you prefer to use the mirror as a table decoration, place a few tea lights or a pillar candle in the middle of the arrangement and sit the whole thing in the centre of your table.

TOP TIPS

- Remember that plants and flowers grow in clusters, so it looks more natural to have groups of your dried nuts and seeds together, rather than individual items scattered around.

- Instead of varnish, spray your arrangement with whatever colour of paint you like.

- To add some sparkle to your arrangement, put all your ingredients into a plastic bag and spray both silver and gold paint into it. Close the bag, shake and the contents will be beautifully coated in a mixture of colours. Leave to dry before you start glueing them to the mirror.

Gift Crafts

We all love receiving gifts. In fact, I enjoy the moment of unwrapping almost as much as seeing what's inside. Delicately removing the ribbon, easing aside the paper, opening the box ... I get excited just thinking about it.

If I'm honest, though, I get even more pleasure in giving presents, especially when I know I've got it right and the recipient will be absolutely thrilled.

Since I started meeting and learning from inspirational crafts people, I've turned over a new leaf when it comes to gifts. I now try to avoid shop-bought extravagances in favour of the homemade and personal. I think making a gift for someone is one of the nicest things you can do. It's unique, something that nobody else in the world has, and shows you have made a special effort. Don't get me wrong: we all put time and effort into choosing a shop-bought gift, but actually making gifts is so much more personal.

What particularly appeals to me about homemade gifts is that you can show some-one how well you know them, their tastes and interests. For example, an embroidery depicting the main events in someone's life makes a fantastic gift for a significant birthday. It's also about passing on a history. I made my son a teddy bear a couple of years ago and I love the fact that he will be able to pass it on to his children in due course.

One of best things about homemade presents is that they save you lots of money. It's true they probably take more time to make than buying shop-bought, but think of all the fun and satisfaction you get in the creation. If you've been hoarding materials, as I've been urging you to do throughout this book, you will have a crafting

box containing everything you need to rustle up a present – fabric, ribbons, buttons, beads, card, pretty paper. You can then browse through the projects in this book and you're on your way.

Scouring second-hand shops for things to customise is another great way of making fantastic, unique presents for friends and family. If you're inventive with what you find and use your imagination when looking through the shelves, buying presents this way could save you a fortune. Yes, it takes time (something that we all have too little of nowadays), but it really is worth every ounce of effort. I'm always popping down to my local second-hand market and I get such pleasure searching for the right item. I don't necessarily find a bargain every time I'm there, but the trick is to go in regularly and something is bound to turn up. Remember, at markets you can haggle, and often the more you buy, the better the deal you can negotiate.

Now let's get down to the practicalities of actually making presents for people. The first step is to choose something that will appeal to the recipient, and this chapter has ideas that are all about indulgence and loveliness. The jewellery projects, for example, are really glamorous, but won't cost you the earth. Like the earliest jewellery, which was made from readily available materials such as teeth, bone, shells, carved stones and wood, ours is made from leaves and buttons. Those early examples were often functional items used to fasten clothes together, but jewellery gradually became a form of adornment, and wealthy people paid artists to produce unique pieces using precious metals and gemstones

If you want to give jewellery-making a go yourself, creating something in silver clay is a good place to start. This amazing material is cheap, pliable, easy to use at home and produces fantastic results. See our two pieces of silver clay jewellery on pages 209 and 213 – I know you'll be impressed because the results are extraordinarily professional.

Smelly things to put in the bath are always winning presents for both women and men, and they've come a long way since the days when soap was considered a luxury item and heavily taxed. Back then, artisans devised their own recipes, which they handed down from master to apprentice. With the Industrial Revolution came advances in

production, and in 1853 the tax on soap was repealed. The soap industry flourished as never before, and received an odd boost when dynamite was invented that same year. Nitroglycerine, a waste product of soap-making, is an essential ingredient of the explosive. Who'd have thought it?

Today there are still artisans who use traditional methods of making soap and related smellies. Jenny Elesmore is one such person, and gives her recipes for bath creamers and bath bombes on pages 203 and 205. Try them once and you'll never buy from the high street again.

While relaxing in a beautifully fragranced bath, I think it's essential to have candles in the room. They completely change the atmosphere, making the business of washing something far more glamorous. They are also really easy to make and decorate yourself – page 215 explains all.

It's said that smell is the most powerful of our senses, and a sniff of something can instantly transport us to the time and place we first encountered it. Boiled cabbage inevitably evokes memories of schooldays, but your mother's perfume can waft you back to the cosiness of sitting on her lap when she read you a bedtime story.

Fragrances for personal use were once restricted to the wealthy, but in 1874 the first synthetic aroma chemicals were invented, and perfume became accessible to all. Nowadays it's a multi-billion pound industry, and while it might be accessible, this doesn't mean it's a cheap gift. The great news is that you can create your own scent (for yourself or someone else) and it won't cost a fortune. For the secrets of making scent for a fraction of the cost of shop-bought fragrance see page 199.

Whatever present you've opted to make, it's really important to wrap it beautifully because anticipation is a huge part of the pleasure. Tissue paper, ribbon, buttons and bows all help to make the gift feel luxurious and special. But rather than reusing something from your craft box, why not make a simple ribbon rose (see page 195)? It's another indication of the care and effort you've put into making someone happy, and that's what this chapter is all about.

❧ Ribbon Rose ❧

Making a gift look pretty by adding special finishing touches to the wrapping is one of my favourite things to do. There are so many great ways to go about it, and with very little effort you can make your gift look fabulous. Even if you are wrapping a gift in the most basic brown paper, adding a beautifully tied bow can transform it from boring to beautiful. Have a go at this stunning ribbon rose, which I showed some fellow WI members how to make, and give your gifts the wow factor.

YOU WILL NEED

- Wire-edged ribbon, whatever length and width you want, depending on what size of rose you want to create
- Pins (optional)
- Needle and thread

1. Pull 10 mm of wire from one side of the ribbon and secure by bending it backwards or poking the end through the ribbon.
2. Gather the ribbon along the side where you pulled the wire. It will curl up as you do so.
3. To create the centre of the flower, roll up one end of the ribbon as tightly as you can.
4. As the flower gets bigger, bend the ribbon outwards and further away from the centre. You can adjust the shape as you go and pin it together if you like.
5. Once the whole piece of ribbon is rolled up, sew together at the back of the flower shape to hold it in place, making sure you stitch the centre tightly to maintain its shape.

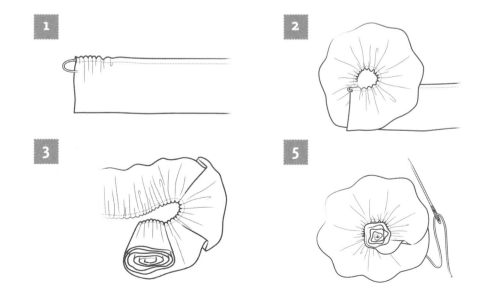

Making Perfume

I absolutely adore perfume. It's a very personal statement, and spraying some on as I leave the house makes me feel completely ready for the day. I was lucky enough to make my own scent, fragrance 'K', with expert perfumier Sally Hornsey. She explained how the fragrances are grouped into five main categories: floral, green/fresh, fruity, oriental (spicy or sweet), and woody. The individual smells are then divided into different 'notes' – top, middle and base. When you smell a perfume, it is the top notes you connect with first, followed by the middle notes, and finally the base notes, which hang around the longest.

To Make Fragrance 'K'

Sally helped me to create my own blend of oils, and all for under a fiver.
(JLo and SJP eat your hearts out!) But you can easily do it at home too. Here's how …

YOU WILL NEED

- Pipettes (one for each fragrance oil used)
- Fragrance oils: bergamot, coconut, honey, rose
- Measuring beaker, preferably with a lip for ease of pouring
- Perfumers' alcohol
- 50 ml perfume bottle with spray attachment
- Mini funnel (optional)

All the oils and equipment needed for this project are available from specialist suppliers and easily found online.

1. Using separate pipettes, measure the fragrance oils into the measuring beaker. You will need 1 ml (30 drops) bergamot; 1 ml (30 drops) coconut; 1 ml (30 drops) honey; and 4 ml (120 drops) rose.
2. Add 43 ml perfumers' alcohol, then gently stir the liquids together to ensure they are blended properly.
3. Pour the liquid into the perfume bottle. This is easiest using a mini funnel, but it's also possible with a lipped beaker. Spray and enjoy.

To Make Your Own Fragrance

Choose a selection of fragrance oils, making sure you have at least one top note, one middle note and one base note oil (see chart below). You can use oils from the same family, or a combination of families.

YOU WILL NEED

- Cotton wool pads
- Paper plates
- Your chosen fragrance oils
- Pipettes (one for each oil used)
- Measuring beaker, preferably

with a lip for ease of pouring
- Perfumers' alcohol
- 50 ml perfume bottle with spray attachment
- Mini funnel (optional)

TOP NOTES	MIDDLE NOTES	BASE NOTES
Apple (fruity)	Bay (green/fresh)	Amber (sweet oriental)
Bergamot (fruity)	Basil (green/fresh)	Benzoin (sweet oriental)
Clove (spicy oriental)	Cherry (fruity)	Chocolate (sweet oriental)
Ginger (spicy oriental)	Coconut (green/fresh)	Frankincense (spicy oriental)
Grapefruit (fruity)	Cucumber (green/fresh)	Honey (sweet oriental)
Lime (fruity)	Geranium (floral)	Jasmine (floral)
Mandarin (fruity)	Lavender (floral)	
Neroli (fruity/floral)	Lilac (floral)	
Orange (fruity)	Mango (fruity)	
Petitgrain (fruity/woody)	Rose (floral)	

1. Place a cotton wool pad on a paper plate and carefully add a drop of your chosen top note. Using a fresh pipette, add a drop of your middle note, then wave the pad in front of your nose to smell how the oils combine together. Using another pipette, add your base note and test the smell again.

2. Adjust the perfume blend by adding a few more drops of whichever smell you want to be most prominent. Between one and five drops of oil should be enough. You can play around until you get the right fragrance, but try to keep the amount of drops to a minimum.

3. Keep a note of how much of each oil you use so you can work out proportionally how much you need to fill your perfume bottle. It takes 7 ml oil + 43 ml perfumers' alcohol to make 50 ml perfume. The key thing to remember is that 1 ml oil = 30 drops, so to make 7 ml oil you need 30 x 7 = 210 drops in total.

My fragrance on the cotton pad had:

Bergamot	1 drop
Coconut	1 drop
Honey	1 drop
Rose	4 drops
Total	7 drops

To work out the proportions needed for my perfume I divided 210 by 7 and got the answer 30. Each drop on my cotton pad therefore equalled 30 drops in the perfume, as follows:

Bergamot	1 drop on cotton pad x 30	= 30 drops in beaker
Coconut	1 drop on cotton pad x 30	= 30 drops in beaker
Honey	1 drop on cotton pad x 30	= 30 drops in beaker
Rose	4 drops on cotton pad x 30	= 120 drops in beaker
Total	210 drops	

4. Once you have decided on your mix of fragrance oils and are happy with the blend, you will need to make up 7 ml (210 drops) of the mixture using the formula given in step 3. Put this in a measuring beaker and add 43 ml perfumers' alcohol. Stir gently, then pour into your bottle.

TOP TIPS

• The best perfumes are made from essential oils, which are concentrated extracts from plants. It takes at least 30 whole flower heads to make just one drop of rose essential oil, so a 10 ml bottle can set you back £80.

Fragrance oils are much cheaper, between £2 and £5 for a 20 ml bottle, but the scent does not last as long.

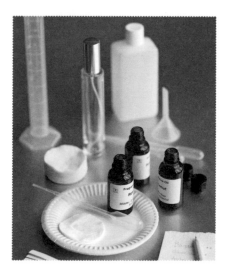

❧ Lavender Bath Creamers ❧

Plop a bath creamer into the tub the next time you're getting in and it will leave your skin feeling soft and moisturised, just like a baby's. Creamers make wonderful presents for your nearest and dearest, especially if wrapped in tissue paper and placed in a beautiful box with a bow on top. Using this recipe by Jenny Elesmore, give them on their own or make them alongside the bath bombes (page 205) for a double whammy of gorgeousness.

YOU WILL NEED
....

- 100 g cocoa butter
- 50 g shea butter
- 50 ml almond oil
- 2–4 ml lavender essential oil
- Small paper cases for moulds
- Rosebuds

1. Put the cocoa butter in a plastic jug and microwave on High for about 20 seconds, until melted.
2. Add the shea butter to the jug and microwave again until that has melted too.
3. Stir in the almond oil and lavender essential oil, then allow to cool for a few minutes.
4. Arrange the paper cases on a tray. Spoon the mixture into the cases and leave to become cloudy and cool (about 10 minutes).
5. Once the creamers are cloudy, insert a rosebud into the centre of each one. Set aside for 24 hours, and the creamers are then ready to use.

Lavender Bath Bombes

I adore smelly things. Whether it's a rich body lotion, something scented for the bath, or a refreshing shower gel, there is no more indulgent or personal gift that you can give.

I met Jenny Elesmore a few years ago when she taught me how to make my own soap, and believe me when I say it went down a storm with my family and friends. Here she shares her recipe for delicious bath bombes that will give any bath that special bit of fizz. The quantities below make about four bombes.

YOU WILL NEED

- 450 g bicarbonate of soda
- 300 g citric acid granules
- 150 g cornflour
- 2½ tsp lavender essential oil in a spray bottle
- 4 large bombe moulds that divide in half
- Sunflower oil
- Pinch of lavender buds
- Bulldog clips

All the equipment for this project can be bought online from any soap-making website.

1. Sift the bicarbonate of soda, citric acid and cornflour into a large bowl, then mix well.
2. Gently spray two shots of the lavender oil thinly and evenly onto the flour mixture and stir together. (The mixture will bubble and swell, so proceed with caution.) Repeat this step carefully until the mixture just about holds together like wet sand when pressed firmly between your fingers. (This needs less oil than you think.)
3. Grease your bombe moulds lightly with sunflower oil, place some lavender buds in each one, then pack the oil mixture firmly into both halves. Press together and hold together with a bulldog clip. Leave the bombes overnight to harden.
4. The following day, open the moulds and use a twisting action to remove the bombes; they should be firmly set in a ball shape. Leave them for another day to dry completely, then they are ready to use.

Silver Button Medallion

Receiving a beautiful piece of jewellery must be one of the nicest gifts ever. It's a truly personal and thoughtful present, and will always have a special meaning because of its associations with the giver. That connection is all the greater, though, when the piece has been carefully handmade. The maker has poured all their love and imagination into it, and the receiver will treasure it forever.

Jewellery-making is a great and accessible craft, but don't assume that pieces made at home have to be confined to beads and cheap wire, or that sophisticated items require special training. Put your preconceptions to one side and let me introduce you to silver clay. This magical ceramic substance contains tiny particles of silver mixed with cotton fibres and non-toxic binder. Once the clay is modelled and dried, it's fired on an ordinary gas hob, where the fibres and binder burn away to leave pure silver. No specialist silver-smithing is required, and most of the tools needed are probably lying around your house (any others are very affordable and available online). The result is a beautiful, handmade piece of silver jewellery that can even be hallmarked.

I was shown how to use silver clay by jewellery designer Emma Mitchell, who uses it to create the most beautiful, tactile and wearable one-off pieces of jewellery inspired by her vintage finds. I love searching for and hoarding old buttons, so this project uses a button as its inspiration.

YOU WILL NEED

- Glazed tile or granite/ marble block or large flat plate or other non-porous work surface
- Drop of cooking oil
- Craft knife or non-serrated kitchen knife
- 2–4 g Art Clay Silver 650, Slow Dry
- Rolling guides, 2 mm thick (2 plant pot markers stacked either side of your oiled area are perfect)
- Small plastic rolling pin or a thick marker pen
- Circular cutter, about 2 cm diameter (the narrow end of an icing nozzle could be used instead)
- Thick needle
- Plastic button, slightly smaller than the cutter, with large buttonholes and 3D detail, such as a ridge around the edge
- Baby wipe or piece of dampened kitchen paper, folded several times
- Fine needle or pin
- Firing gauze
- Camping stove (optional)
- Tweezers
- Small metal polishing brush
- Art clay silver sanding pads (optional)
- Pliers
- Silver jump ring, 5–6 mm in diameter
- Silver bracelet or necklace chain

1. Ensure your chosen work surface is clean and dry, then apply a small drop of oil to it and rub it into a small area. This will prevent your silver piece from sticking.
2. Use your knife to cut a 3 g piece of clay about 1 x 1 cm and place it on your oiled surface. Rewrap the remaining clay carefully, putting a drop of water inside the pack to keep it moist for your next project (see Top Tips).
3. Put your piece of clay in the centre of your oiled surface between the rolling guides. Roll into a roughly circular shape as evenly as you can until it is just over 2 cm wide.
4. Press the cutter into the clay and hold it in place while you trim away the surrounding clay with your knife. Roll the spare clay into a ball and put it back in your packet – it can be used for another project.
5. Remove the cutter and poke the thick needle into the top of your clay disc about 2–3 mm from the edge. Press the needle right through the clay to the hard surface beneath and move it in small circles to make a hole about 2–3 mm in diameter. This creates a hole for your jump ring.
6. If you're using a button as part of your design, hold it patterned-side down above the clay disc to centralise it by eye, then push it firmly into the clay.
7. Poke the thick needle through the holes of the button to make corresponding holes in the clay. Carefully remove the button from the surface.
8. Alternatively, if you do not have a suitable button, use your thick needle to make either two or four 'buttonholes' around 3 mm in diameter in the centre of your clay disc.

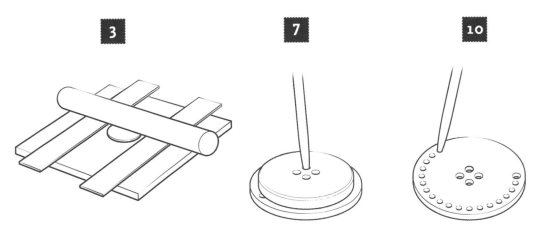

9. Use the pad of your finger to gently flatten any raised areas around the buttonholes you have made in the clay.
10. At this stage you can also use the thick needle to make patterns, such as a row of decorative dots around the edge.
11. Leave your clay disc to dry completely for a couple of hours, then lift it from the work surface (it should detach easily). To speed up the drying process, heat the oven to 180°C/Gas 4 and place your clay disc in it on a glazed tile, baking tin or piece of foil for 15–20 minutes.
12. Hold the disc carefully, supporting the edge with your fingers (it can be brittle at this

stage) and use a folded baby wipe or damp kitchen paper to remove any ragged or sharp pieces from around the edge.

13. Hold the disc up to the light and make sure you can see through the hole you made for the jump ring near the top. If not, place it on a hard surface and very carefully use a sharp pin to open the hole.

14. Place your firing gauze over a camping stove or a hob on your gas cooker. Light the gas, turn it up to its highest level and let the gauze heat up so that one or more areas becomes red hot.

15. Carefully use your tweezers to place the clay disc on one of the red-hot areas of the gauze. Watch closely – a flame will rise up from your disc. Do not alter the heat – simply wait for the flame to die down, then leave the gas burning beneath your disc for another minute before turning it off. This ensures that all the cotton fibres burn away, leaving pure silver.

16. Let the medallion cool on the gauze for 5 minutes. It should look matt white: this is silver oxide on the surface. Hold your medallion firmly and use a wire brush to remove the oxide and reveal the silver underneath.

17. You can leave your medallion with a matt brushed silver finish, or use an Art Clay silver sanding pad to generate a mirror shine on the surface.

18. Use your pliers to open the silver jump ring. Slip it through the hole at the top of the medallion and thread your necklace or bracelet chain through the ring. Close the jump ring, again using your pliers. Your piece of handmade jewellery is finished.

TOP TIPS

• To recycle dry clay, put it in a small ziplock bag, add a couple of drops of water and knead until the clay becomes uniformly soft again.

• If your clay becomes a bit dry while you are still working it, moisten your finger very slightly in water, touch the clay and it should become soft again. Similarly, if you

have to leave your project for some reason, dab a drop or two of water on the work surface near the clay, cover with cling film and it should stay soft for up to an hour.

Silver Leaf Pendant

The crafting competition at the New Forest County Show was one of the most challenging that I encountered, and to complete my three-craft entry on the theme of 'The Secret Garden', I went along with the ladies from the 'Disparate Housewives' WI group based in Twyford to visit Larissa Johnson. Larissa runs The School of Jewellery and Craft and agreed to give us a lesson in the wonderful craft of silver clay. Here she shares her method so you can try it too.

YOU WILL NEED

- Approx. 10 g Art Clay Silver 650, Paste Type
- Leaves – the best are geranium, rose or sage, but use any firm leaf with an interesting shape and defined vein structure; waxy leaves or those with fine hairs are not suitable
- Tile
- Paintbrush
- Stainless steel mesh suitable for gas hob firing
- Hairdryer
- Sponge sanding pad or block
- Steel craft tweezers
- Soft wire brush (stainless steel or brass)
- Burnisher
- Hand-held pin vice and fine drill bit
- Silver jump ring
- Jewellery pliers
- Silver chain, leather thong or ribbon

1. Dilute some clay paste, 2 parts paste to 1 part water (the consistency of single cream). Lay the leaf on a tile with the underside facing up and paint just that side with the mixture.

2. Put the leaf on your steel mesh, painted side up, and dry with a hairdryer. When it is completely dry, repeat steps 1 and 2.

3. Dilute some clay paste to the consistency of double cream and dab it onto the painted leaf quite thickly – this will prevent the first two layers from being pulled off. Dry with a hairdryer.

4. Keep dabbing on layers and drying them until your leaf is about 1 mm thick. (You'll end up with about 4–5 layers.) Leave to dry completely.

5. Using a sanding pad, gently sand away any rough areas and remove any surplus paste that is on the front of the leaf. Be very careful as the pasted leaf is extremely fragile.

6. If using a gas hob to fire the leaf, put the mesh over the gas flames and wait for it to become red. Turn off the gas, then use tweezers to place the leaf on the red area. Turn on the gas again and the leaf will flame up for a few seconds, then turn orange. Fire for 5 minutes, then leave to cool for 20 minutes. If using a cook's blowtorch, place the leaf on a ceramic fibre brick and fire for 2 minutes. If using a kiln, fire the leaf at 800°C for 10 minutes. Cooling can be finished by dipping the leaf in cold water. Dry well.

7. Once fired, use the metal brush to smooth the leaf, then use a burnisher to highlight the edges and the texture. Burnishing will also help to strengthen the leaf.

8. Place the fired, polished leaf on a firm surface. Insert the drill bit in the pin vice and drill a hole in the leaf for attaching a jump ring. Thread with a chain and the pendant is ready to wear.

❧ Decorated Candles ❧

I'm always raving about how much I love candles. My motto is to have them in every room and light them as often as possible, so here's a lovely, straightforward project by Jill Alblas to make your own. Before you start, remember to protect your clothes with an old shirt or apron, and to cover your work surface with papers or an old cloth.

YOU WILL NEED

- 300 g candle-making wax
- 30 g stearin (an acid that improves colour and burning quality)
- Candle dye
- Scissors

- Wick
- Acrylic mould (9 cm high x 6 cm wide)
- Greaseproof paper
- Sticky Tack
- Cocktail stick

- Wax sheets in pink and brown
- 2 paper punches, flower shape and spot shape
- Baking parchment

1. Place a heatproof bowl over a pan of simmering water. Add the wax and stearin, melt together, then add a spot of dye.
2. Trim the wick so that it's 10 cm longer than the height of the mould. Keep hold of one end of the wick and dip it in the molten wax. Straighten the wick between your fingers and place on greaseproof paper to harden.
3. Thread the hardened end of the wick up through the mould as shown below. Seal the wick at the bottom of the mould with Sticky Tack (reusable adhesive). Fix a cocktail stick across the top of the mould and hold in place with Sticky Tack. Take the wick over the cocktail stick and secure with Sticky Tack on the side of the mould.
4. Pour the melted wax into the mould. Place the mould in a large bowl, put a weight (e.g. a tin of beans) on top, then fill the bowl with cold water up to the height of the wax. Leave for about 40 minutes, by which time a dip will have formed around the wick. Remelt the leftover wax, top up the mould and leave to set.

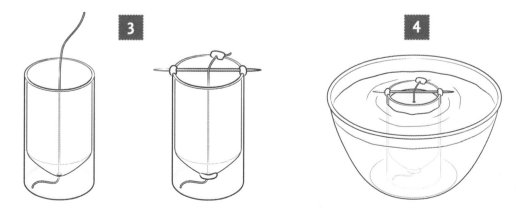

5. While the candle is setting, remove the backing paper from a pink wax sheet and punch out about 18 flowers. Punch the same number of spots from a brown wax sheet.

6. Once the candle is completely set, remove it from the mould.

7. Cut the wick flush at the base of the candle and to about 1.5 cm at the top. Place the candle on a sheet of baking parchment. Firmly press the punched flowers over the candle in the arrangement of your choice. Press a punched spot in the centre of each flower.

TOP TIPS

- For a quick start, remelt some old candles, or melt inexpensive ones from a supermarket. But if you do this rather than using new wax, don't add any stearin to the melted mixture.

- Don't be tempted to speed up the setting process by adding ice to the bowl of water as this will cause the candle to crack and flake.

- Pour any leftover wax into a bowl lined with baking parchment and leave to set. It can then be lifted out and stored in a plastic bag, ready to use again.

SAFETY NOTES

- Never heat wax over direct heat or in a microwave as it can overheat and ignite. Always use a double-boiler.
- Do not leave melting wax unattended.
- Keep lit candles away from draughts, soft furnishings, children and pets.
- If hot wax splashes on the skin, immerse immediately in cold water.

Contributors

The people listed here all made a huge contribution to this book by devising wonderful craft projects. I hope you'll enjoy making them as much as I did.

JILL ALBLAS
Tel: 01945 870975
jillalblas@aol.com
Jill is a highly versatile crafter. She provided the projects for our carved window box, mosaic chair and decorated candles (pages 145, 153 and 215).

SAM BOMPAS
Bompas & Parr
Flatiron Yard
14 Ayres Street
London SE1 1ES
Tel: 020 7403 9403
info@jellymongers.co.uk
www.jellymongers.co.uk
Sam is a superb jelly-maker, who helped me to make the lovely crenellated party jelly on page 121.

LOUISA CARTER
Louisa@louisacarter.com
Tel: 07766 604420
Louisa is a home economist who devised the recipes for ice-cream balls, marzipan penguins and garden pickles (pages 119, 123 and 137).

JO COLWILL
Cowslip Workshops
Newhouse Farm
St Stephens
Launceston
Cornwall PL15 8 JX
www.cowslipworkshops.co.uk
Jo is an expert in needlecraft. She offers an extensive range of fabrics (over 1000 bolts), sewing notions, books and buttons, plus classes and workshops in patchwork, quilting and country crafts.

VICTORIA CRANFIELD
Cranfield Foods
East Down
Barnstaple
Devon EX31 4LR
Tel: 01271 850842
vc@cranfieldsfoods.com
www.cranfieldsfoods.com
Victoria showed me how to make sugar flowers and damson jam (pages 129 and 135). Her company sells a wide variety of preserves,

and I truly believe she is the 'Queen of Condiments'.

ROSIE DAVIES
Penny's Mill
Nunney
Frome
Somerset BA11 4NP
Tel: 01373 836210
info@rosiedavies.co.uk
www.rosiedavies.co.uk
Rosie showed me how to make elderflower cordial (page 149) and a wonderful fruit cake (page 115) that inspired my winning entry to the Devon County Show.

AMANDA DRAKE
Administrator
Redhills Community Primary School
Landhayes Road
Exeter
Devon EX4 2BY
Tel: 01392 255555
Amanda helped coordinate all my little helpers to make the scarecrow on page 161.

JENNY ELESMORE
Odds and Suds
8 Brook Street
Tavistock
Devon PL19 0HD
Tel: 01364 654882
shop@oddsandsuds.com
www.odddsandsuds.com
Jenny makes fantastic things for the bath, and provided the projects for creamers and bombes (see pages 203 and 205).

JAYNE EMERSON
Tel: 07809 142088
jayneemerson@hotmail.com
www.jayneemerson.co.uk
Jayne is a needlefelt expert, the author of 'Simply Needlefelt', published in 2009, and a supplier of needlefelting tools. See page 61 for instructions on how to make her delightful needlefelt robin.

PAUL HAWKINS
www.paulhawkinsflowers.co.uk
Tel: 0870 850 2721
Paul is a floral decorator who makes the most wonderful arrangements. He provided several of the projects in the flower crafts chapter: table centre, garden wreath, corsage and seedhead mirror (pages 179–83 and 189).

SALLY HORNSEY
Plush Folly – Make Your Own Cosmetics
Tel: 07851 429957
info@plushfolly.com
www.plushfolly.com
Sally is a top-notch perfumier who helped me to make my own delicious fragrance, 'K'. The project she provides in this book will help you to make your own scent too (see page 199).

RICHARD HUNT
Executive Chef
The Grand Hotel
Torquay
Devon TQ2 6NT
Chou7x@aol.com
www.grandtorquay.co.uk
Richard is the 'King of Scone-making', and you can try his fantastic recipe on page 133.

ANN & ELLIE JARVIS
Clovelly Silk
Lower Yard
Clovelly
Bideford
Devon EX39 5TL
Tel: 01237 431033
clovellysilk@hotmail.com
www.clovelly-silk.co.uk
Ann and her daughter Ellie are a brilliant team who showed me how to make a beautiful devoré silk scarf. The process is revealed on page 57.

LARISSA JOHNSON
The School of Jewellery & Craft
The Old Barn
Priory Court
Wood Lane
Beech Hill

Berks RG7 2BJ
info@tsjc.co.uk
www.theschoolofjewelleryandcraft.
co.uk or www.tsjc.co.uk
Tel: 0118 988 3200
Larissa is an artist who produces
beautiful jewellery in silver metal
clay. She helped me to make
the stunning leaf pendant on
page 213.

SUZIE JOHNSON
The Wool Sanctuary
Weston-super-Mare
Somerset BS23 3BH
susiejohnson1@btinternet.com
www.thewoolsanctuary.com
Suzie is a hand knit designer with
a passion for colour. She runs her
small hand knit business from
home and provided the project for
bubble coasters on page 39.

HELEN MELVIN
Fiery Felts
Blaen Wern
Waen
Bodfari
Denbighshire LL16 4BT
Tel: 01745 710507
helenmelvin@fieryfelts.co.uk
www.fieryfelts.co.uk
Helen is an artist who produces
amazing pictures made from fibres
and fabrics she dyes herself. She
reveals the secrets of using natural
dyes on page 67.

LINDA MILLER
www.lindamillerembroideries.co.uk
Linda is a wizard at machine
embroidery and showed me how to
use this craft to make an appliqué
rose for a pretty patchwork cushion
(see page 21).

JAINA MINTON
jaina@polkadotsundays.com
www.polkadotsundays.com
Jaina is a paper sculptor who turns
old newspapers into beautiful
works of art. She showed me how
to make the lovely sculpture bird
on page 79.

EMMA MITCHELL
Tel: 01638 741063
emma@minniedog.co.uk
www.emmamitchelldesigns.co.uk
Emma is a jewellery maker who
uses silver clay combined with
enamel and semi-precious stones to
make sewing- and nature-inspired
pieces. See how to make her
vintage-style silver clay medallion
on page 209.

SARAH MORPETH
Tel: 01830 520350
sarah@sarahmorpeth.com
www.sarahmorpeth.com
Sarah is an artist who makes
amazing books and works in cut
paper. See how to make her
paper bauble on page 93.

ANNEMARIE O'SULLIVAN
www.annemarieosullivan.co.uk
Annemarie works wonders in willow,
producing traditionally crafted
items that are a joy to own. Find out
how to make her willow nesting box
on page 165.

CHERYL OWEN
Cherylowencrafts@aol.com
Cheryl is a whizz at making handmade paper (page 99), and has lovely
ideas about how to use it. See her
delightful scrapbook on page 103.

EMILY PEACOCK
Digit Design,
PO Box 4153
Bourne End
Bucks SL8 5FY
Tel: 07964 734978
tapestry@emilypeacock.co.uk
www.emilypeacock.com
Emily is a needlework designer,
specialising in contemporary cross-
stitch. She designed the fabulously
quirky sardine cushion on page 45.

PHIONA RICHARDS
www.rarenotions.co.uk
rarenotions@hotmail.co.uk
Phiona is a book sculptor and paper
artist, who produced the elegant
paper bead necklace on page 83.

SIONED ROWLANDS
Tulipa
tulipa@tiscali.co.uk
www.tulipaflowers.co.uk
Sioned is a very talented floral
designer, who showed me the ropes
for making a petite exhibit for the
Cornwall County Show. See page
175 for the lovely result.

MANDY SHAW
37 Summerheath Road
Hailsham
East Sussex BN27 3DS
Tel: 01323 845297
mandy@dandeliondesigns.co.uk
www.dandeliondesigns.co.uk
Mandy is an amazing crafter, who
turns her hand to so many things.
She provided the projects for
bunting, the stack and whack quilt,
paper dolly chain and snowman
piñata (pages 17, 41, 87 and 89).

TAN STRONG
Greenacre House
Parrott's Lane
Cholesbury
Near Tring
Herts HP23 6NY
Tel: 01494 758926
tanstrong@hotmail.com
www.tanstrong.net
Tan is an award-winning flower
arranger – a gold medal winner
at the 2010 Chelsea Flower Show,
no less – so do try her classic line
design on page 185.

AMANDA WALKER
Dedham Hall Business Centre
Brook Street
Dedham
Essex CO7 6AD
Tel: 01206 322690
Amanda@thesoftfurnishingstudio.
co.uk
www.thesoftfurnishingstudio.co.uk
Amanda is an embroiderer par
excellence, producing work by hand
(see the handkerchief, page 29) and
by machine (see the stylish table
runner, page 33).

Suppliers

The best crafters are also magpies, collecting useful materials wherever and whenever they clap eyes on them. Scraps of fabric, chocolate box ribbons, giftwrap, buttons, silk flowers, glitter, paper, card… nothing goes to waste if they have their way. Does that sound like you? If not, please start right now to build up a collection of bits and pieces that you can plunder whenever inspiration strikes. Of course, there'll come a time when your craft box doesn't contain exactly what you want, but that doesn't mean you have to rush out and spend lots of money buying what you need. Jumble sales, charity shops and car boot sales are great places to pick up lovely stuff very cheaply. But when even they fall short, you will need to buy from specialist suppliers – and that's what this list is all about. It contains the contact details of suppliers that our expert contributors recommend, and also includes some of the big online companies. Search, find and craft!

BUTTONS AND HABERDASHERY
http://efco.sinotexuk.com for buttons and sequins.
www.macculloch-wallis.co.uk for trimmings and sewing notions.
www.vvrouleaux.com for a variety of ribbons.

CANDLE-MAKING
www.candlemakingsupplies.co.uk for wax, moulds and much more.
http://efco.sinotexuk.com for mini cutters.

CLAY
www.cooksongold.com for silver art clay and related tools.

CROSS-STITCH
www.embroiderywool.co.uk for Appleton Brothers crewel wool.
www.willowfabrics.com for canvas, needles and crewel wool.
www.zweigart.com for tapestry canvas.

CUSHIONS
www.thefeathercompany.com sells bespoke cushion pads made to any shape and size you want.

DÉCOUPAGE
www.decoupatch.co.uk for découpage paper, brushes and glue.

DEVORÉ
www.homecrafts.co.uk for devoré paste.
www.lawrence.co.uk for silk screens and squeegees.

DRIED FLOWERS AND PETALS
www.devonpressedflowers.freeserve.co.uk
for pressed flowers.
www.scentedhome.co.uk for dried lavender.

EMBROIDERY
www.bernina.co.uk for information about sewing machines and embroidery.
http://franklins.directknitting.co.uk for machine embroidery thread.
www.james-hare.com for silk fabric suitable for table runners.
www.johnlewis.com for a wide range of needlecraft supplies and fabrics.
www.therange.co.uk for hand embroidery threads, needles and hoops.

FELTING
www.dandeliondesigns.co.uk for fabric, patterns and a wide range of haberdashery.

JEWELLERY-MAKING
www.cooksongold.com for silver art clay and related tools.
www.palmermetals.co.uk for jewellery findings in gold and silver.
www.spoiltrottenbeads.co.uk for beads and jewellery findings.

KNITTING
www.thewoolsanctuary.com for wool, needles and lots more.

MOSAIC
www.creative-distribution.co.uk for mosaic glue.
http://efco.sinotexuk.com for tiles and grout.

NATURAL DYES
www.dtcrafts.co.uk for mordants and yarns.
www.jennydean.co.uk for dye information and workshops.
www.pmwoolcraft.co.uk for dyes and mordants.
http://scottishfibres.co.uk for fibres and yarns suitable for dyeing.

NEEDLEFELT
www.fredaldous.co.uk for felt, feathers and fleece.
www.hobbycraft.co.uk for needlefelting tools.
www.texere-yarns.co.uk for yarns.

PAPERCRAFT
www.bladerubber.co.uk for rubber stamps.
www.creativememories.org.uk for a wide variety of papercraft supplies.
www.docrafts.com for a wide range of crafting supplies.
http://dovecraft.com for card, paper and scrapbooking materials.
www.paperchase.co.uk for paper and card.
www.papermania.com for royalty-free images to use on cards, etc.

PATCHWORK
www.cowslipworkshops.co.uk for a huge range of fabric, buttons and threads.

PERFUME-MAKING
http://sensoryperfection.co.uk for fragrance oils.
www.fragrancesforall.co.uk for fragrance oils.

QUILTING
www.antiquequiltsandtextiles.co.uk for vintage textiles, old ribbons and buttons.
www.cottonpatch.co.uk for all quilting needs, including 'fat quarters'.

SOAP-MAKING
www.thesoapkitchen.co.uk for all soap-making supplies.

WILLOW
www.musgrovewillows.co.uk for British willow supplies.

WOODWORK
www.dremel.co.uk for woodworking tools.

Index ✂

KIRSTIE'S ACKNOWLEDGEMENTS

This book was born out of the hard work and talents of numerous brilliant crafts people who have taught me a thousand and one new things. You all know who you are: without your patience and guidance, none of this would be possible.
I am also very thankful to all my country show rivals, whose competitive spirit has pushed me to up my game and take my love of crafts to a whole new level.

If I am still alive today, it is no thanks to Sarah Walmsley and Lisa McCann at Raise the Roof, who are responsible for driving me to challenge myself and, in the process, creating a competitive craft monster. They were aided and abetted by Jane Muirhead, Chrissie Butler, Julia Bird, Laura Harding, Laura Wiseman, Ellie DeCourt, Holly Sandford, Laura Knox, Alan Stanley, Sarah Sarkhel, Martyn Bon, Sinead Dockery, Kathryn Burnett, Louise Scrivens, Deborah Dunnett, Jonny Wharton, Anne McCargo, Stephanie Hutchinson, Michelle Reece, Richard Poet, Ollie Hulbert, Jim Dunbar, Ian Garvin, Cliff Evans, Melvin Wright, Ed Bulman, Jean Pierre Bassin, Jon Boast and Daniel Russell.

They were all egged on by the wicked masters at Channel 4 – Kate Teckman, Andrew Jackson, Sue Murphy, Clemency Green and Hanna Warren.

I have Jane and Sarah to thank for finding the only person who couldn't travel the length and breadth of the country making crazy TV (because she was having twins) and giving her the task of bringing all the madness together in a book; Jeannot you are a true saint, and so is Fiona Murray, who was so sweet and patient when taking pictures.

I am very grateful to Hodder for getting involved with all this madness again. Thanks to Nicky Ross, Trish Burgess, Sarah Hammond and the team.

And the same applies to everyone at BBC Worldwide, who had faith that Phil and I could be in charge, with the right minders, of course.

My agent Hilary, at Arlington Enterprises, is heroic, as is the home team of Katharine, Jamie, Heather, Maravic, Angelina, Chrissie and Sophie, who have remained calm in the face of numerous requests, demands, photo shoots and missing items. Thank you one and all.

PUBLISHER'S ACKNOWLEDGEMENTS

We would like to thank Fiona Murray for her photography. Thanks also to Cole & Son (www.cole-and-son.com) and Claire Coles (www.clairecolesdesign.co.uk).

First published in Great Britain in 2011 by Hodder & Stoughton
An Hachette UK company

6

Copyright © RTRP 2011

A CIP catalogue record for this title is available from the British Library

ISBN 978 1 444 73758 5

Photography © RTRP Ltd
(except pages 28, 31, 32, 38, 40, 44, 56, 58, 64, 66, 71, 86, 88, 92, 96, 98,
101, 102, 105, 107, 114, 118, 119, 120,122, 124, 128, 131, 136, 144, 152, 156, 164,
178, 180, 182, 188, 201, 202, 203, 204, 205, 208, 212, 214, 216)

Text editor: Jeannot Hutcheson
Project editor: Patricia Burgess
Step-by-step illustrations: Kuo Kang Chen
Photography styling: Cynthia Inions
Home economist: Louisa Carter

Typeset in Mrs Eaves and Nexus

Printed and bound in Great Britain by Butler Tanner & Dennis Ltd

Hodder & Stoughton policy is to use papers that are natural, renewable and recyclable
products and made from wood grown in sustainable forests. The logging and
manufacturing processes are expected to conform to the environmental regulations
of the country of origin.

Hodder & Stoughton Ltd

338 Euston Road
London NW1 3BH

www.hodder.co.uk

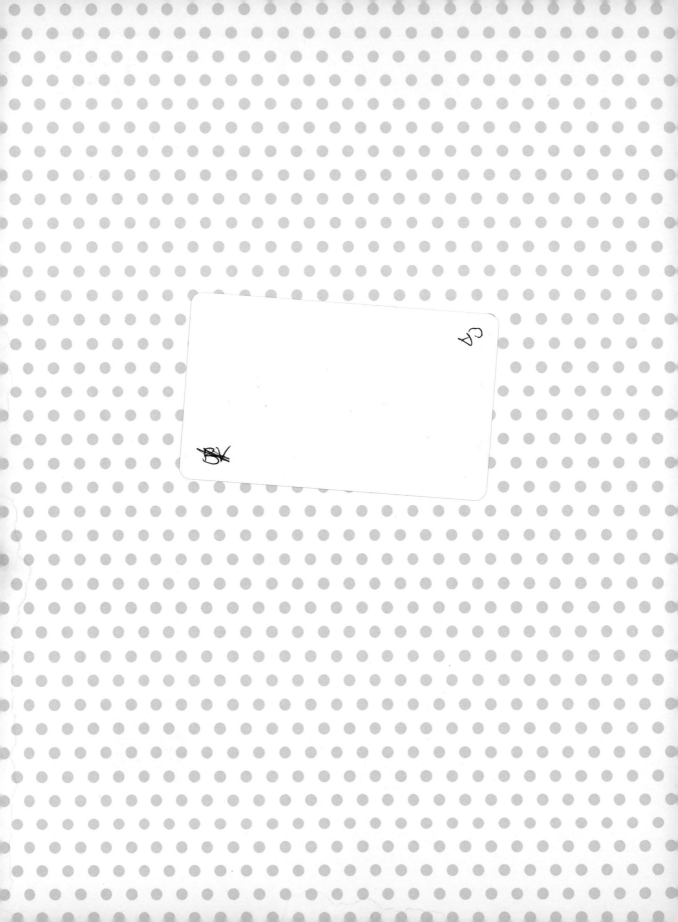